think. create. sell.

think.
create.
sell.

The Insider Secrets
Your Best Friend Would Tell You
About Entrepreneurship

CAROL O'BRIEN

ISBN: 978-1477444641

www.cleanicity.com

*For my husband who has somehow
stayed sane—and kept me sane—on this crazy ride.*

Contents

Introduction

Congratulations! You have a really great product idea!

It may be an idea that you've been thinking of for years. Or, one you came up with after you had a life-changing event. Maybe, it's something you've been looking for and when you couldn't find it, you decided to create it.

Most likely, you have mentioned it to your family and friends and more than one has said, "That's a great idea! I wish I had thought of that."

Regardless of how you came up with your idea, you have just become an inventor.

Now, don't be surprised. Inventors are people who come up with ideas. Not all of them make a million dollars, but some do. Not all take their idea through to production, but some do. Not all bring products all the way to the marketplace, but some do. The bottom line is that each inventor started with an idea.

And you have one!

It's very exciting. But now what? Every entrepreneur has started where you are now. They didn't start out as savvy businesspeople who knew exactly what they needed to do every step of the way. They believed in possibilities. And the successful ones learned to harness their passion to create breakthrough products.

And you can, too.

This book is for all aspiring inventors, licensors, and entrepreneurs who have a big idea and a dream to make it a reality, but don't know what to do next. You may be going it alone—for now. Once you read this book, you'll see you're not alone at all.

Come along with us and see if this ride is for you.

Chapter 1:
The Big Idea

There are a ton of incredibly innovative, brilliant ideas out there that never become a reality.

There are a ton of not-so-extraordinary ideas that go on to make millions of dollars.

What's the difference? While there are many factors involved in the long-term success of a product or service idea, such as available financing and the grit and determination of the entrepreneur, let's stay with the idea for now.

Ideas that solve real problems win.

It sounds simple enough, but what does that really mean? The key word is "real." And real is in the mind of the consumer, not the inventor. Imagine that you are a seasoned tennis player. You've come up with this phenomenal idea for a new tennis racquet for beginning tennis players that replaces the nylon strings in most amateur racquets with a brand new material that improves performance, reduces injury, and increases durability.

These sound like great problems to solve, right?

The question is: does the average new tennis player see these as problems? More specifically, would a new tennis player likely buy a tennis racquet that promises to solve these problems? Amateur tennis players often buy their racquets based on which brand they know, or on price. Even tennis experts recommend that amateurs focus on head size and length to maximize their early command of the ball.

To sell your new tennis racquet to beginning players, first you would have to convince them that they need to be worried about performance, injury, and durability. And then, you'd need to compete with bigger brands on any number of things including price, shelf space, promotions, and more.

It's infinitely harder to convince your customer that there is a problem than to solve an existing problem with a great new product.

So, you need to assess your idea with a critical eye. A good place to start vetting your product idea is to ask yourself three questions:

- *Is my product brand new or does something similar already exist?*

- *If something already exists, does my product offer a better way?*

- *Does anybody want or need a better way?*

Searching on Google is an easy first step to see if your product idea exists. You can also browse through the shelves of a Big Box or specialty retailer who sells products like yours. While you may be tempted to do your research completely online, if you have the time, visit the stores in person. You'll get a feel for how many products are in your space, how consumers buy product like yours, how competitors package their products, and how retailers stock the shelves in your category.

Remember that your competition is more than products just like or similar to yours. Your competition is any product that the consumer buys instead of yours. Say you sell a specialized child's hair brush that does wonders with detangling a child's hair. Your direct competition is other brushes that may or may not offer detangling features. Your indirect competition is a detangling shampoo that provides similar benefits. And your very indirect competition, but one who still competes for your customer's dollars is the barber down the street who keeps a child's hair short and free from tangles.

If you find something very similar to your product, don't panic. There's a reason that the phrase "build a better mousetrap" is in our vernacular. Ask yourself that second question again, "Does my product offer a better way?" If so, you are in a good situation. You know that there is a market for your product; otherwise retailers wouldn't be carrying something similar. And you know you have a better solution for the competing product's customers.

Answering the question, *"Does anybody want and need a better way?"* is a little hard to answer by yourself. Because you saw a need for it, it's easy to assume that everyone does. The next sections will help you look at your idea more objectively.

Don't Fall in Love:
Lessons from the Journey

I received a piece of advice from a veteran entrepreneur that I'll never forget. He said, "Don't fall in love with your idea."

I didn't understand what he meant. How could I *not* fall in love with it? This idea was keeping me up day and night with excitement. I spoke to all of my friends about it. I already knew it was going to be a lot of work to take it from an idea to a reality, so why shouldn't I love it from the get-go?

After a few months and several thousands of dollars invested, I finally understood.

Here is the background. I had an idea swirling around in my head for years. It was patiently waiting there for me to get around to implementing it.

When I was laid off in 2009, my big idea finally had its opportunity to shine. I had been working as a marketing executive and because it was what I knew, I started interviewing for the same kind of position. *In the middle of an interview*, it hit me. I just couldn't do this anymore. I didn't feel the passion for my career anymore. It all felt stale and depressing. I needed to do something else.

Luckily for me, I knew what I wanted to do. I wanted to give my big idea its chance. My husband was working, but we would be going from two incomes to one. With my husband's income, though, I felt a little bit more comfortable about taking a risk. Perhaps that safety net made me less diligent than I should have been. I forgot what I knew and had been taught, and went ahead with my big idea without truly vetting it first.

I had seen sticky mats in cleanroom environments years before. These mats are made with sticky adhesive layers that peel off when the top layer is soiled. They are positioned outside cleanroom doors so that workers step on them prior to entering a sterile environment. The mats take the very last bit of dirt and debris off workers' shoes, so they don't bring contaminants into the room.

After seeing them, I just knew they would work in households, too. As an aspiring clean freak, I dreamed of days where dirt no longer tracked into my house from the shoes of my husband, kids, family, friends, neighbors, and pets. I knew I could make those sticky mats into a product—a fashionable, sticky entrance mat—to help keep homes across America cleaner.

I forgot to ask the "new Coke" question—does anybody want or need a better way? They might think my entrance mat is a cool idea but do they really need it? Do they really want it? And maybe most importantly, will they drop their current product and buy my better, cooler entrance mat?

After working with a manufacturer to revise the mat for new materials, color, and sizing, investing in a production run, launching a Web site, setting up a merchant account, and kicking off a marketing campaign, the answer was pretty clear. The people I was reaching out to were just fine with their existing entrance mats.

They didn't have a *need* for a different or new kind of mat because they weren't having any *problems* with their old one. My big idea had had its day and it failed.

Well, not quite. We'll get into that a bit later.

The lesson I learned is that assessing a product idea—with people who might actually buy the final product—is a critical step in launching your product or service. In addition to finding out if anyone wants or needs your product, you need to know how much they would pay for it and how it compares to competing products.

Embrace the Research

How do you begin vetting the idea? Well, if you have $100,000 to invest, I'd say go to the best market research firm you can find and have them put your idea in front of potential customers. Don't have $100,000? Then $20,000 will get you a pretty good market research firm. Don't even have that much?

No worries–you're in great company! Most inventors pay for their fledgling products themselves (which is called "bootstrapping") and prioritize spending on product development and advertising.

As you'll see in the next session there are creative ways to assess your product or service idea without spending a fortune.

7 Tips for Market Research on the Cheap

Especially if you're bootstrapping your product idea, it's easy to convince yourself that you don't need market research.

Don't fall for it.

Before you go head first into production, you need to understand your customers and how they will respond to your offering. Market research can help you answer many critical questions such as: who is your target audience? What needs do they have? What existing products are solving their problems? Will your product do a better job? How much will your audience pay for your product?

Again, if you can afford to hire an advertising agency or research firm to test your product or service idea, it will provide insights and expertise that are hard to match on your own. But that doesn't mean you can't do a good job of it yourself. You just have to be clever.

You've already determined if your product is brand new or a better solution than an existing product. Now try some of these inexpensive tips to get important insights into your customers and your market before you spend your first dollar. What you learn may help you reshape your big idea into an even bigger idea!

TIP 1. Get a good understanding of your industry.

I started with this one to remind you to begin looking at your product from a bigger perspective. Your product will be part of an industry of products and that industry will impact how well your product does. Take an automotive product for example. Say you've found that the air inside large SUVs doesn't circulate as much as in smaller cars, so you've created a product that helps move the air around better while purifying it at the same time. Great idea! What if you learn that the sales of SUVs, though, are expected to decline sharply by 2015 and car companies will be phasing them out, starting now? You wouldn't have to scrap your idea. But, having that information might help you revise your target audience or industry altogether, maybe you market your product for airplanes or buses instead.

A good place to begin gathering information on your industry is with industry monitors. Published by research firms, these reports provide valuable information about whether your industry is growing, how big your segment is, the key players, and more. Some of this research can be quite expensive, but you may be able to find full reports or snapshots of your industry online. Your local library or alma mater may provide free access to subscription services that carry these full reports, too. Examples are: IBIS World industry reports (IBISWorld.com has good industry Report Snapshots where you can glean valuable information before you have to pay for the full report); Euromonitor International; and Hoovers industry reports.

Another place to look is on your industry association's Web site. Most of the associations will provide industry sizing and trending information for free.

Insider secret: You may find a research report that looks like it has everything that you need but it is too expensive and you don't have access to it through a library or other option. Type the name of the report into Google. Try it with quotes first, for example, "2012 xyz industry trends." Reporters or bloggers often receive industry reports and write articles or blogs on them. You may be able to extract the exact statistics and commentary you need from those media sources. If nothing comes up with quotes, try your search without them. A writer may not have used the full name of the report in his or her article.

When you are researching your industry, the questions you want to ask include the ones below.

How big is the industry?

You want to know if your industry is robust or if it is on the smaller side. If it's large enough, you can start breaking it down to the size of your subsegment. For example, annual spending on the Fashion and Accessories Industry is approximately $250 billion in the US. Its subsegment, Handbags, Luggage, and Accessories, is a $9-billion industry. You have a pretty healthy industry to be able to introduce a new product into if you just break the industry down to handbags.

In contrast, another fashion subsegment is Hats and Caps, which is a $2-billion-dollar industry. It is dominated by products for men with nearly 60% of the sales, followed by women's and children's products. If your product is a woman's hat, for example, you can start to see that your segment within the fashion industry is relatively small. You would want to research further to gauge whether or not you will be able to effectively and profitably introduce a new product into the market.

Is the industry projecting growth?

In tough economic times, consumers tend to stop spending money on things they don't consider necessities. When consumers stop spending, whole industries are impacted and the size (i.e., both the number of companies in the industry and the revenue generated by the industry) may decline sharply. Now, if your industry is growing or even staying relatively flat, especially in these current economic times, you can guess that customers see products in your industry as a necessity. And the definition of "necessity" is in the cash of the beholder. Take the pet industry as an example. It is considered recession-resistant because typical pet owners may cut down on what they buy for themselves, but not on supplies, toys, and accessories for Fido!

Knowing whether your industry is growing or shrinking can help you think about your product differently. Say you're an amazing knitter with a big idea to use specially spun silicone fiber into a sweater for women. You learn that spending on women's clothing in the US has declined by 1.1% in the past five years and is expected to continue declining. At the same time, you learn that spending on children and infant's clothing in the US grew by 0.4%, and is expected to continue growing.

You may decide to rethink your women's sweater and make it a sweater for toddlers. Or, you may decide to research the women's clothing industry further to see if the decline in spending is only expected to last as long as the recession. In that situation, you might decide to keep going with your original idea. In either case, knowing what's happening in your industry is critical as you continue thinking about and shaping your big idea.

Is it concentrated?

If your industry is concentrated, it means that a few large companies hold most of the market share—and the trust and dollars of your potential customers. The large companies' big dollars can mean it is difficult for a small company to come into that space and compete effectively. That's not a hard and fast rule, though. With an exciting new product, your small company can take away some customers from the big guys, or even expand the market altogether—meaning customers will buy from you *in addition* to buying from the larger companies.

If an industry is not as concentrated and the large players don't hold a lot of the market share, it is likely an industry with lower barriers to entry. That means that companies are able to more easily enter the industry. Less well-known brands can introduce new products and win over customers. It also means there are many more companies competing with you.

Consider this example: you have a patent on a voice-activated car-mirror system. Maybe the automotive parts industry in the US is very concentrated. Suppose, as an example, that there are four big companies and they pretty much own the US market. Further suppose that the market in Europe is not as concentrated so many more companies can get in easily. If you don't have the budget to effectively market to both countries, where do you plan to sell your product?

You may decide to sell it in Europe because there you don't have to be a major brand to get onto automotive retailers' shelves. Or maybe, you decide that the competition is too great in Europe and that all of those small companies' products will make it hard for your product to get noticed. Perhaps your product is so unique and desirable that you know US automotive retailers won't care that your brand isn't well known yet and take a chance on you. You could also consider licensing your product to one of the bigger players.

How big is the target market (i.e., the people who might buy your product)?

Some inventors create products that only appeal to a small number of potential customers. That's not a problem if your product is very costly and only a few sales are needed to make the profits you desire. Most of the time, though, inventors make products that have very low margins, meaning the amount of money you get to keep after subtracting the cost to make and sell the product. Especially if you work through a distributor or a retailer, your profits may only be a few dollars. So you'll need to sell your products to a large number of people to make your profits count.

To find the number of your potential customers, first decide who is likely to buy your product.

- What is their gender? Men, women, or both?
- Where do they live?
- What is their education level?
- What is their income level?

Now ask for whom they are buying your product:

- For themselves for personal use?
- For a family member?
- For the family as a whole for common use?
- For a pet?
- For someone else?

Then ask why they are buying your product. Try to articulate the need or want in very specific words. You may not know all of the answers yet, but you are starting to develop a profile of your potential customers. Keep coming back to these questions as you develop your product.

What are the biggest trends in the industry?

Watching trends is a great way for smaller companies, with smaller dollars, to break into an industry. If your product features and benefits align with what's hot in the industry, you're already well on your way to winning customers. If it doesn't, take another look at your product. Is there a way to adjust it or add to it, so it better meets the needs and desires of your customers?

Narrow in on Your Product

Now that you have a good overall perspective of the size of your industry and its trends, begin narrowing in on your specific products and potential customers.

TIP 2. Read reviews of competing products online.

Online reviews are goldmines of information because they'll tell you what real buyers like and find lacking in current offerings. Many online reviews enable customers to rate a product's quality, value for the money, durability, and more. Especially if customers feel that competing products could be better, online reviews can help you create your product in ways that address what's most important to your potential customers. Even the research to find competing products will yield valuable information. You'll discover which retailers and Web sites carry products like yours. Check out Amazon.com, Walmart.com, Target.com, and others for a wide range of general products and the feedback from customers. If you're thinking of a more specialized market, go to online merchandisers in your segment and see what their customers think of existing products.

Tip 3. Conduct your own focus group.

If you're creating a product based on something you need and can't find it's a good bet that the people you associate with may be in the same boat. For example, if you're a computer programmer who sees a need for an ergonomically correct armrest, your coworkers are probably computer programmers with arm strain, too. Get a group of friends, family, and co-workers together in person to talk about your idea. Sure, in the beginning they'll all say it's a wonderful idea, but dig deeper and ask specific questions. Be sure to listen with a critical ear—you'll be surprised by what you learn!

Tip 4. Facebook or Google+ your friends or key connections.

Hold virtual focus groups with friends, family, and coworkers who are not close enough to join an in-person discussion. Keep in mind that social tools may share your product ideas with the general public before you're ready if you're not careful. With the new features of Facebook and Google+ you can easily limit the views of your posts to just the people you want to see them. Share your product idea and ask for genuine insights from your connections.

Tip 5. Ask the social world for feedback.

Several sites, like LinkedIn and WordPress, let you create online polls. If you're comfortable sharing your idea, ask your group members or followers to give you specific feedback including how much they'd pay for your product. If you're not comfortable sharing your idea just yet, you can mask it by asking what your group members or followers like or don't like about what's currently available.

Tip 6. Check out SCORE or other startup associations and ask them for feedback.

SCORE started out as the "Service Corps of Retired Executives." The organization counsels small businesses and their mentors can help you put a magnifying glass on your product idea. Your mentor will assess your idea from an experienced businessperson's perspective. And, if you make the decision to move forward with your idea, he or she will provide you with inexpensive training and free mentoring on starting and growing your company.

Tip 7. Visit an industry trade show.

While displaying in a trade show can be quite expensive, attending one is usually a lot cheaper. This is especially true if you don't have to travel to the show and just have to pay the price of admission. There are a few types of trade shows; the ones you'll be interested in are shows for end customers of products like yours or shows for retail buyers in your industry. By attending either of these, you can gain a lot of information about what types of products are hot and what consumers or buyers are looking for right now.

All of this information will help you start forming an understanding of your market and the people to whom you will be selling.

As a bonus—you'll be able to use the information you gather for your business plan that we discuss in Chapter 3!

A Real-Life Example: How I Used Inexpensive Market Research for My Own Product

After my big idea's short life, I still had many thousands of dollars invested in a product that wouldn't sell. To help me figure out what to do, I conducted an idea group with family and friends. From that one brainstorming session, we came up with the idea of the Stikitty®. We'd revise the sticky entrance mats into an adhesive cat litter mat—that is, if the market needed it, wanted it, and would pay for it.

I was adamant I wasn't going to make the same mistake twice.

Before I took one step, I decided to start with my target audience. Answering the target audience questions from earlier in this chapter for my product idea, I learned:

- Both men and women are likely to buy the Stikitty®, but more women than men buy cat products

- They live in the US, currently, but people all over the world would likely buy my product

- Their income is moderate and up

- They are buying it for their family for common use in the house

- They are buying the Stikitty® because they have a cat and they don't like cat litter tracking all over their houses

So, my target market is US cat owners. I can find out from the American Pet Products Association that 38.9 million US households own cats. I might be able to narrow this a little further if I knew how many of these cat owners have a cat litter box instead of having outdoor cats that don't use one. Even so, I can see that my target market in the US is a good size. As the Stikitty® expands and I start exporting it, I will look at the countries with the highest number of households with cats, and my other target market characteristics, to determine which countries will have the most potential customers.

Next, instead of trying to convince myself and others that the Stikitty® was a good idea, I started from the opposite perspective. I told myself that the world didn't need another cat litter mat. I did full-time research for weeks and used the inexpensive market research resources I mentioned above to see if I could prove my negative hypotheses. I knew that if I could prove them, my idea wouldn't stand the test of time—or a limited budget!

Below are examples of my negative hypotheses and what I found through research:

The Pet Industry is Saturated & There's No Room for Growth

Through my alma mater, where I had alumni access to online library resources, I was able to gain electronic access to industry overviews, articles, and snapshots on the pet industry. I found the Datamonitor and IBIS World reports especially helpful. In addition to industry information, I looked at the strategic and financial performances of key companies.

I found that the $45-billion pet industry has grown for the past seven years and it is projected to grow for the next five, albeit at a slower pace. There are extremely large competitors but the industry is fairly fragmented with the top companies commanding only ~35% of the market. New companies are able to thrive with strong branding and good sales strategies.

People Only Spend Money on Dog Products

Through networking, I connected with a retired, high-level executive from a leading international pet company. He told me it's true, that the biggest chunk of my $10-billion pet supplies subsegment goes to the dogs; specifically to dog toys, collars, leashes, and more. However, when cat owners spend, they spend big on litter and litter supplies—to the tune of nearly $2 billion annually.

No One Wants a New, Different Kind of Cat Mat

This hypothesis was critical—if I could prove that no one needed or wanted a more advanced cat litter mat, I would have to stop right there. Because I knew direct customer insights were crucial and I couldn't afford formal customer research, I used the tips above to "hear" from as many cat owners as possible. So, I:

- Conducted dozens of in-person focus groups with family, friends, and neighbors with cats; I asked them about their current litter mats and what they'd like in a new solution

- Visited large and small pet retailer Web sites to read on-line reviews of cat litter mats

- Lurked on pet forums to learn of frustrations about cat litter tracking and possible solutions

- Polled contacts in my LinkedIn pet groups

- Sent samples to friends, and friends of friends on Facebook, and asked them for their feedback on the Stikitty® and how I could make it better

What I Learned from the "Negative Market Research"

I learned that the pet industry is more recession-proof than others and it is projecting growth; that cat litter products are a strong segment within this very large industry; and, that cat owners are eager for a lighter, easier to clean cat litter mat that is the right size for their specific needs. I found that cat owners were open to something different and, if it solved their issues with traditional litter mats (e.g., too heavy, too hard to clean, not large enough), they would buy something innovative. Additionally, I found a lot of practical information, such as, how to price my product, which retailers carried competing products, and how to package and display the Stikitty®.

Though I wasn't able to completely fool myself, looking at my product idea from a negative perspective allowed me to listen to my head. I was able to step aside and bring my future customers' needs and desires to the forefront. I was able to look at things from a business perspective.

4 Things to Do Right Now

So, you've now done your market research, listened to your head, your friends, and your potential customers, and tested your hypotheses. You've found an idea that solves a real problem and you've vetted it objectively. You're pretty sure you're ready to move forward. You're ready to launch your product, right?

Not quite yet.

Having a potentially winning idea is a great start, but there are other things to consider. I've chosen four tips from my favorite entrepreneur friends on what to do before launching your company.

1. Set a time limit and then forget it.

Upfront, determine how much time you're comfortable taking to see if you can make your idea work. This time might be a period away your career or changes in your schedule that impact your kids or spouse. Is it six months? A year? Once you have set a comfortable time limit, put that worry aside and get down to business. If you don't do this, you'll constantly be looking in the rearview mirror. You'll think, "Look at all this time I'm wasting. I should be looking for a different or new job; I should be spending time with my kids; I should be doing…" any number of things. But, if you give yourself permission to focus for a length of time on your idea and then promise yourself not to feel guilty about it, you'll be able to spend your energies on the positive actions needed rather than the negative obstacles that could hold you back.

2. Define a Go / No-Go budget and stick to it.

Calculate how much of your own money you'll be able to invest in giving your idea a go. Even if you get outside financing, investors or the bank will expect you to use a portion of your own money. When you've reached your budget limit, take a critical look at what you have learned. Make the hard decision about whether or not to continue. You may even decide you need to change course and push your idea in another direction. By setting the budget limit, you'll do two things. First, you'll spend your precious dollars wisely; and, second, you'll stop worrying about the costs because you've already earmarked that money as money you will invest. If you get to your limit and decide not to go forward, the least you've done is learned a lot along the way. If you do decide to go forward, you will have made a wise initial investment in the potential of your product.

3. Find a sounding board who is not your best friend or your mother.

Objective advice is critical when starting and building your own company. You don't need "yes" people around you; you need people who will ask you the tough questions. Again, SCORE is a great option here. They have experienced mentors and valuable resources for startups and most of their services are free. It's a comfortable environment for you to share your business idea. They'll ask you questions and push you to think harder. If you find a mentor who you'd like to share this journey with, they'll share their time with you for free. If they can't help, they'll point you to someone who can. What a great organization!

4. Learn to listen to your gut.

A friend of mine, Aly Benson, inventor of the Whippy Clip™, said to me that her biggest mistakes so far have happened when she didn't listen to her natural instincts. Starting on this product journey is new for most of us, so sometimes we allow ourselves to be intimidated by the newness of it all. We start to question our decisions and listen to people who may not know how to be helpful and effectively encourage us. So instead, they become naysayers. At these times, listen to your gut. Your instincts and your integrity have brought you this far and both are critical tools to bring with you on this journey. Keep them close.

The Big Idea Checklist

- ❑ Determine if you have a product that solves a real problem

- ❑ Learn about your product's industry

- ❑ Research the competition and their products

- ❑ Conduct in-person and virtual focus groups on your product idea

- ❑ Find a no-nonsense sounding board

- ❑ Visit an industry trade show

- ❑ Assess your product using "negative market research"

- ❑ Set a time limit and a go/no-go budget

- ❑ Listen to your instincts.

What Would You Tell Your Best Friend About... LAUNCHING?

What would I tell my best friend if she were thinking of launching a product? I would first ask her three questions: Is there a need for your product? Is there a market for your product? Would you use your product? If she can answer "Yes" to all three, I would encourage her to move forward.

Kathy Baker, Founder
Vanity Fixes, Inc.
www.bralief.com

My best friend is also my pastry-chef, so she has heard all of this already, but what I would tell her about launching a product is: Go for it! Take every skill you have and figure out how it can help build your business, come up with an amazing, unique idea and get out there.

Mari Luangrath, Founder
Foiled Cupcakes
www.foiledcupcakes.com

Chapter 2:
If You Knew Then…

Now that you have a product idea fully vetted, and ready to go, you have an important decision to make. It's about how you're going to bring your product to market and which path is going to make you the happiest.

Recently, I asked Aly Benson what advice she'd give her best friend if she wanted to start a company. Aly said:

> *I'd tell my best friend that if your heart is in this and you have a passion for business, marketing, and sales, and not just inventing then this could be a very exciting process. You need to do a whole lot of soul searching first because it takes guts, hard work, and money.*

Aly's passion lies in the process of coming up with ideas that solve problems. And she came up with a really good one. She invented the Whippy Clip™, an adorable, animal-faced suction cup that attaches to any flat, non-porous surface. It has multiple straps to keep your child's toys, sippy cups, and pacifiers within easy reach and off the floor. Parents love the idea as it provides thirty minutes of sanity at meal time.

Aly's passion does not lie in manufacturing, marketing, sales, and financials. The good news is it doesn't have to. The fortunate thing about living in these wild, wild Internet days is that there are paths for every type of inventor. Choosing which one is right for you is critical before you begin the process.

The Inventor

in·ven·tor: a person who invents, especially one who devises some new process, appliance, machine, or article. *Source: Dictionary.com*

If, like Aly, coming up with ideas is right up your alley but taking on the production end bores you to death, then being an inventor may be your path. Notice that I didn't say "scares" you to death. The manufacturing, marketing, financial, and legal aspects of a business scare just about everyone who hasn't done them before. But, if you have absolutely no desire to take on the responsibility of a business, you have other options. Web sites like EdisonNation.com, Quirky.com, and newcomer AHHHA.com allow inventors to submit their product ideas to an online Web site for a small fee. If your idea is chosen by the crowd, the inventor site will take it, produce it or have a sponsor produce it, sell it into retailers, and market it for you. You will receive royalties for as long as the product sells.

If you'd like to be a bit more hands on, there are several organizations that can help. For a fee, these inventor helpers will guide you through the process of getting patents all the way to taking products to market. Caution: scamming inventors out of money and their ideas has been a calling for criminals for a long time. The US government even offers resources to help the inventor sniff out scams before any money is exchanged.

Pros of Inventing Only

If you're an idea person and that's all you want to do, it's never been easier to see your product idea come to life. You don't need much capital outlay to submit your idea for consideration. If you are selected, it's a great way to earn passive income.

Cons of Inventing Only

Even if your idea is a good one, there is a lot of competition, especially if you're using the crowd sites. There is no guarantee that your product will be selected. Also, with the minimal capital outlay comes minimal return on investment in terms of royalties. And you have to be very cautious about scammers.

The Licensor

li·cen·sor: someone who grants formal permission for someone to do something, as to carry on some business or profession. *Adapted from: Dictionary.com*

Some inventors with a really good idea and no desire to start a business decide to go the licensing route. This means selling your product idea to another company to have them manufacture and sell it. Often, you may need a working prototype to sell your idea to the manufacturer. In exchange for your idea, typically you will receive 3-10% in royalty fees on the wholesale price. (The wholesale price is the price that the manufacturer charges the retail store. The retailer then adds their mark up and that becomes the retail price. See more on this in Chapter 6.).

Often, manufacturers who buy product licenses have relationships with retailers or distributors already in place. Therefore, the manufacturer is in a good position to be able to turn your idea into a reality and then sell it to retail partners in a short period of time.

Insider secret: If you choose to license your product to a manufacturer, be sure to have your lawyer add in a "guaranteed minimum" clause into the contract with the manufacturer. This clause says that the manufacturer has to sell a certain number of your products in a certain amount of time. If they don't, then they've lost the right to license your product and you can take it to someone else.

In the not too distant past, the inventor had to approach each of the manufacturers separately and make a licensing pitch. Now there are Web sites popping up all over that connect you to interested manufacturers or sponsors. For a fee, you can submit your product idea and manufacturers or funding sponsors can view your idea to see if it matches their needs. It also works in the opposite direction. Manufacturers and sponsors can post what they're looking for, so inventors like you can submit your idea directly to the requestor.

In addition to virtual networking of manufacturers to inventors, these Web sites often offer training and resources to walk you through the licensing process. Check out EdisonNation.com and other similar sites.

One thing to know ahead of time is that many of these Web sites require you to have a patent or a pending patent to submit your idea. That's a catch-22 for most inventors. When manufacturers get their hands on your product, they may have suggestions or ideas to change the product and make it better. If you have submitted your patent application already and hadn't included the specific iteration of the idea, the ultimate product may not be covered under your patent. If the inventor-networking site allows for it, your best option may be to file a provisional patent application where you will still be able to make changes before you file for a non-provisional patent. (See more about this in Chapter 4).

If you decide to speak to manufacturers directly and don't have a patent, you can partially protect your product idea with a non-disclosure agreement (NDA). NDAs are legally binding documents that say that the parties involved will not share any of the information that is covered by the NDA with anyone else.

Manufacturers are very familiar with NDAs and typically sign them without hesitation. If your manufacturer won't sign one, think twice about sharing your idea with them. My lawyer prepared my NDA for a small fee; there are some good templates on the Internet as well.

Pros of Licensing

If the process of bringing a product up to the prototype stage excites you, but taking it further holds no appeal, licensing can be a good middle of the road option for you. The capital outlay may be a bit more than inventing only, but considerably less than full-on entrepreneurship. It offers better returns than inventing only, too.

Cons of Licensing

The biggest con for you may be ownership. You've nurtured your big idea all the way to the prototype stage; can you hand it off to someone who doesn't love it as much as you do? If the answer is yes, then licensing is definitely the path for you. You won't get to keep as much of the profits as the entrepreneur, but you also won't have as much of the work and the risk.

The Entrepreneur

en·tre·pre·neur: a person who organizes and manages any enterprise, especially a business, usually with considerable initiative and risk. *Source: Dictionary.com*

The definition of an entrepreneur varies greatly from that of an inventor. That's because the entrepreneur is one who takes on the full job of making a *company* not just a *product*.

Because this book is about how to launch your product, it focuses on product inventors and entrepreneurs. It is worth taking a bit of time to explain the difference between product and service entrepreneurs as sometimes people confuse the two. Service entrepreneurs make most of their income when they are actually working. People pay them for their expertise and typically they bill their clients by the hours they've worked or in a lump sum for a consultation, coaching session, or training seminar. Product entrepreneurs make most of their income *after* they've done the work. Once you've launched your product, gotten it to your channel of distribution, and marketed it, the job is now in the hands of the customer. Most of your investment and labor occur upfront before you earn a penny, hence the riskiness of being a product entrepreneur.

There are many reasons entrepreneurs want to manufacture and market products themselves. Firstly, you have the benefit of being involved in your product's journey all the way to the end customer. It can be very gratifying to see what you created on store shelves or in the hands of customers. Secondly, your gross profits will likely be the highest as an entrepreneur, as opposed to an inventor or licensor. That's because, in most cases, you get to keep between 35% and 100% of your gross profits, depending on which channel(s) of distribution you choose. That's a lot different than 2-10% of royalty fees. Additionally, you've already established your channels of distribution, garnered the needed resources and made the necessary relationships to launch a product. Now you're in a great position to keep launching new product ideas.

Pros of Entrepreneurship

As an entrepreneur, you get to see your product all the way to the finish line. Profits are likely to be higher as an entrepreneur, and you're set up to reuse your resources and channels to launch additional products.

Cons of Entrepreneurship

The entrepreneur's path is a lot harder and riskier because the majority of your financial and labor investments are up front. If you don't enjoy the day-to-day work of an entrepreneur, then you may be better off choosing another option.

The Starting Line

It's important to ask yourself if running a business is really what you want. You don't have to enjoy all aspects of the business, but you should be excited about more than just your product. As a former marketing professional, I love the marketing aspect of my job as much as I love coming up with new ideas for products. I sometimes enjoy doing the financials. I will admit it is more fun now that money is flowing the right way.

Don't fool yourself into thinking you can outsource or hire an employee right away to do the more mundane or arduous tasks. If you're like most startup businesses that don't have outside funding, you may need to give your company a year or two to make enough money to support additional employees. In the meantime, if you do want to run your company but decide one aspect of it is really not for you, you can hire a Virtual Assistant. From bookkeeping to answering phones to posting on social sites for you, it seems that there is a Virtual Assistant available for just about any job these days. Some are better than others and you do need to learn how to work effectively with yours.

While running your own business is undoubtedly a lot of work, most people are scared off by it because they think it is an 18-hour a day or more endeavor. As a product entrepreneur, I haven't found that to be the case. On the contrary, for me there have been a lot really busy times and then some really slow times while I'm waiting on product runs or for others to accomplish specific tasks related to getting the product ready to sell.

Especially in the beginning, inventory runs were difficult to gauge. I didn't have the cash to order huge production runs of the Stikitty®, so I ended up with a lot of starts and stops. For example, I'd get inventory in and do a lot of marketing and then I'd run out of product. The problem was I didn't have the cash to do another production run before I sold the product. I'd have to stop marketing while I was waiting for more product inventory to come in. It went on like that for several months until I landed my first distribution deal.

Now because I have a fulfillment center for my Internet sales, I am beginning to outsource some of my marketing, and my distributors do most of the sales efforts with retailers, I have more time again. Now, I'm focusing on launching two new pet products, oh, and writing an ebook!

If You Knew Then... Worksheet

Why does coming up with new ideas excite you?

1. _____

2. _____

3. _____

Why does product development excite you?

1. _____

2. _____

3. _____

Why does running a business excite you?

1. _____

2. _____

3. _____

You may not know all of the answers yet, but if there is a section you are particularly struggling with, revisit this page after reading the rest of this book. See if you can find where your passion lies.

What Would You Tell Your Best Friend About... WHICH PATH TO TAKE?

Know what you really like to do, and determine your business model based on that. When you start a product business, everything is new and exciting. Learning often is. But tasks that were once novel soon tarnish and your business can become drudgery.

Clare Kumar, President
pliio™
www.pliio.com

An idea is not a product and a product is not a company. If you don't have the capacity to do everything required to conceive of an idea, develop and protect a product, and form, fund and run a company (keeping in mind that most people don't have all these skills), you need to be ready, willing and able to work with others to realize your dream of getting an idea to market. To be successful, you need to be honest about what you can do well, and obtain help from experienced others who can do well what you cannot.

Richard C. Bulman, Jr. Esq.
Bulman Business & Technology Law
www.bulmanbusinesslaw.com

Chapter 3:
Getting Started

Even though you may not have begun developing your product, you're well on your way to making it a success. Getting started includes important planning to ensure you're ready to launch your product.

You'll notice that many sections in this chapter begin with "start." That's because you may not have all of the information you need to sit down and complete the tasks at one time. It's okay because the process will help you identify which information you still need to find.

Start Your Business Plan

When most people hear the words "business plan," their first thought is, "ugh." There are good reasons for it as the business plan can be a mammoth, arduous document that often is considered a waste of time by those who have to prepare it. It doesn't have to be that way, though.

Let's start from what the business plan is and what it is not. A business plan is typically a 25- to 35-page document that provides an overview of your company. It is not a static document to be done once and forgotten. You'll understand that the first time you start filling out the plan. There will be many things you may not know yet (like your Cost of Goods Sold, which we discuss in Chapter 7) that you'll have to come back and fill out.

At the very beginning, the business plan is your aspirational vision of what your company could be and how you think you can get to that point. Typically, a business plan includes the following sections:

1. Executive Summary
2. Business Description
3. Market/Industry Definition
4. Products
5. Marketing and Sales Plan
6. Management Team (which may just be you!)
7. Financials

Insider secret: Your first version of the business plan may only be 10-15 pages.

There are several online templates that will guide you through the process. The good news is that you've already started to gather some of the important data you need for the plan during the vetting process for your idea. You'll gather more when you speak to manufacturers and vendors about costs, which you'll use for your financial reports in the plan. And, the remaining chapters of this book will help you answer some of the other sections.

Most small companies only prepare a business plan when they are meeting with investors or bankers. That's because they're often the only ones who will ask for it. However, the business plan is a great way for you to clarify your vision of the company and start to ask the tough questions about your target customers and your competitors.

One last plug for the business plan: Be sure to at least take a stab at filling it out because it can be a very strong tool for your business as you grow. And if a potential partner asks for it, you'll be that much farther ahead. You might even find you enjoy it!

Start Finding Mentors and Taking Training Sessions

I can guess that you're eager for information and guidance on launching your product, which is why you're reading this book. I read as many books on entrepreneurship as I could, too. The challenge I found is that many were focused on the theory of entrepreneurship or on giving inspirational advice on how to hang in there when the going got tough. Additionally, most of the books I read assumed that every startup will become a big, multi-million-dollar business or that my only goal for starting a business was to become wealthy. Other books were older and lacked information about critical technology advances and social media tools that make starting and doing a business today so much different than even a few years ago.

That's why I am writing this book. My goal is to give you the most up-to-date, streamlined information that you need to get started. I promised myself I would tell you everything that I would tell my best friend if she wanted to launch a product. And that's why I'm telling you that you really need to get a good mentor. Mentors provide a sounding board for you about your product and your target audience and can help you stay focused on what is critical to be doing right now. And they may have important contacts to introduce to you.

Your mentor doesn't have to be an academic or an industry-leading expert; she or he just needs to have been where you are right now. There are a great many mentors and coaches out there, but if they are only able to give you general business advice you may be better off saving your time and money. It would be like going to a podiatrist for a toothache. Sure the podiatrist is a doctor, but not the kind you need. You need someone who has launched a product; if it's a product in your industry, all the better!

Your mentor may be paid or unpaid. To find one, start with the big industry—does your product fall into consumer products, medical devices, technology, etc.? Look for a list of mentors and coaches with experience in that bigger classification. Then, narrow down your list to see if you can find a mentor or coach in your subsegment.

Some of the coaches for entrepreneurs offer advice on their blogs and on regular teleseminars. Be sure to sit in on a couple of those, both for the information they provide and to see if you like the coach. That way, if you decide to pay for his or her coaching services, you'll have a good understanding of what that coach brings to the table.

Many organizations also offer training courses specifically for entrepreneurs. Some are generic business ones, like "how to start your company" or "marketing your product 101." These are great courses to take and often are not very costly. Additionally, you may make connections with professionals like lawyers, bankers, or CPAs who you'll need soon.

Other training sessions are more targeted and may be really valuable once you get a bit further along on your journey. But, wait on those until you learn more about your business and the specific training you need to grow. If you take those sessions too soon, it would be like starting your graduate degree before receiving your undergraduate degree. You might not be ready yet to implement what a more advanced training session recommends for you. Additionally, many of the more advanced courses are expensive. So, be sure to wait until you are really ready before you plunk down your precious cash.

For me, the right time for a more advanced course was after testing the Stikitty® on the Internet for several months with a good response from customers. Once I had some successes and had taken a few hard knocks, I took Kim Lavine's course called "Get Your Product into Big Retail Stores." Kim is the author of Mommy Millionaire and inventor of the WuVit, which she sold in large department stores. Her course helped me prepare for what have been my most successful and lucrative sales meetings for the Stikitty®.

Immerse Yourself in Your Industry

In Chapter 1, you researched your product's industry and found important information about its size and robustness. Now, if you are new to your industry or haven't already jumped in with both feet, you will want to start becoming an expert so you can relate to your customers.

The easiest way to dive into your industry is to read updates and articles from multiple sources that provide industry information. The thing about being an entrepreneur today is that the information you need is easily accessible.

It's almost too accessible and can be overwhelming.

The good news is that most information providers allow you to segment and filter the information you receive. Use the filters to keep current on specific aspects of your industry (e.g., marketing baby products to new mothers). LinkedIn has over 700 groups devoted to the pet industry and pet professionals. By belonging to even a few of the groups, I get to listen in on and participate in discussions affecting companies like mine or even potential customers. (Just because I was curious: there are 3,480 LinkedIn groups devoted to fashion!).

Insider secret: Do join groups with entrepreneurs like you and people interested in your industry, but don't forget to join groups that include your potential customers, too. Frequently, those audiences do not overlap.

Twitter is also a great way to stay connected to your industry. Some smart Tweeters have created "best of" lists for every industry, so I only have to click once to get access to a group of people tweeting and sharing links about my industry.

I haven't found Google+ as helpful for following industry information just yet. But I'm sure that will change soon.

Once you start immersing yourself in information about your industry, you'll soon begin to become an expert on hot trends, key competitors, and more importantly, what your customers want, need, think, and feel. And, with this information, you'll have your marketing messages ready even before you get your product prototype!

Time for Your Business Structure

You'll want to take the next step of getting your business registered. That's because you're going to start spending money, if you haven't already, and it's time to consider some financial and legal aspects of your business. Another reason you have to set up your business now is that you're going to have to start paying (or at least deducting) income and sales taxes. Which type of business you choose indicates how you will pay your income taxes. See more on this below.

If you've taken the training courses listed above, then thinking about setting up your business is probably not as scary as you once thought. You may have even met a small business lawyer who is willing to help you along the process. Most lawyers offer a one-hour free consulting session. Take full advantage of the free session by preparing ahead of time. Write down all of the questions you have about which business structure is right for you and any other legal concerns. For example, you'll want to know the legal and tax implications of each business structure, what your state requires in terms of registration, whether your industry requires licenses or permits, whether or not you should consider business insurance, and the answers to any other questions you may have.

While your accountant typically won't give you advice, your lawyer is there to do exactly that. Be sure to ask for the advice you need.

If you don't have a good rapport with the lawyer starting with the free consultation, look for another one. You don't owe the first lawyer anything. Unless you have unusual circumstances, you may not see your lawyer very often, but it is still important to like and trust her or him.

The reason you need a lawyer to help figure out your business structure is that there are a lot of convoluted twists and turns that make it difficult to understand. There are really good resources that provide important details about business structures, but I wanted to give you the basics, so you have an idea of the questions to ask your lawyer. It really is more complicated than I make it out to be below, so promise me that you'll discuss all of the options with your lawyer.

Sole Proprietorship (You)

A sole proprietorship just means that you're not a corporation and you own the business by yourself (or with your spouse in certain states). The government sees your business as "you" so you'll pay your taxes and take deductions as you normally do, on your individual tax form (1040) with potentially a few additional forms for your business. Any profits from your business are taxed as if they were your income.

Your sole proprietorship cannot exist separately from you, typically meaning that you cannot sell your business or even pass it on to your children.

If you want to name your business something other than yourself, in most states you need to file something called a, "Doing Business As." Some states call it a different name, but this filing allows you (remember the government sees your business as "you") to legally do business under a fictitious (not "you") name.

Your personal assets and liability are not as protected as a sole proprietor as they would be if you choose a liability limiting option. If someone brought legal action against you, it would be against "you" and could impact your personal assets. With a corporation, legal action is typically brought against the entity (unless you, personally, acted criminally).

So, why would anyone want to be a sole proprietor as opposed to a corporation? Well, you don't have to file as much paperwork and if your company doesn't make it, it's much easier to dissolve a sole proprietorship. There are other benefits, which your lawyer can discuss with you. Then, you'll have to weigh the pros and cons to determine which is right for you.

Corporation (Not You)

If your business is a corporation, it exists separately from you. The business can be just you or a group of people. By incorporating, you are now consider a "shareholder" and have a limitation of liability. That means the entity is responsible for the debts it incurs and the legal actions it takes. You're not personally responsible, but that doesn't mean you're off the hook if you do something illegal!

In terms of taxes, you have a few choices. For C corporations, the government sees the business as a separate taxpayer. That means there are completely different tax documents for the corporation than for you as an individual.

That's one of the downfalls of C Corporations for small businesses. They experience a double tax. The profits of the corporation are taxed. Then, when the profit is split up among the people who are shareholders, it is taxed again. Unfortunately, in this case, shareholders don't get to deduct any losses from the corporation, but do get taxed on the distributed profits. Because of this, some small companies choose to register with the IRS as S Corporations (see below).

Partnership (A Group of You)

If you have a group of people who would like to share in the profits and liabilities, you can form a partnership. Owners of the partnership are called, you guessed it, "partners." Partners are taxed at their individual personal-tax levels, which makes it easy and straightforward. Also, partnerships can be set up relatively easily with the help of a lawyer. General partnerships do not provide the limitation of liability that corporations do, though.

Limited Liability Company (Not to Be Confused with a Corporation)

There is also a business structure called a Limited Liability Company (LLC) that exists at the state level. The LLC is like a chameleon in that, depending on how you and your lawyer set it up, it can look like a corporation, a sole proprietorship, or even a partnership at tax time!

LLCs are a little confusing because many people, like me, sometimes slip and call them a limited liability *corporation*. However, the LLC is distinctly not a corporation. It is *like* a corporation in that it limits the liability of its owners and it is *like* a sole proprietorship or a partnership in that it allows the owners to pass through income to their taxes.

The owners of the LLC are called members and your tax treatment may depend on the number of members you have.

S Corporation (Just to Confuse You Further)

Sole proprietors, LLCs, partnerships, and smaller corporations can register with the IRS as an S corporation. By choosing to be designated an S corporation, your business can avoid the double taxation mentioned above for C corporations. That's because your business doesn't have to pay income tax on its profits; profits and losses are passed onto the owners to report on their own income taxes.

Not every business qualifies to be an S Corporation. There are restrictions on the number of shareholders you can have and on whom can be a shareholder.

The reason that S corporations get confusing is that the collective "we" (minus the lawyers, accountants, and IRS) tend to mix up state and federal domains. If you remember that your business structure (i.e., sole proprietorship, LLC, partnership, corporation) is defined at the state level and your federal income tax designation (i.e., S & C corporations) is defined at the federal level, you'll be at least half-way toward understanding this! You may need your lawyer and your accountant to get you the rest of the way toward understanding business and tax structures.

What Should YOU Be?

While I obviously can't give you legal advice, I can tell you most of my friends that have small businesses are LLCs. Many also register with the IRS as S Corporations. Because everything depends on which state you are in (or which state you elect to incorporate in) and how you want to handle your taxes, your best bet is to sit down with your lawyer and accountant and determine what is right for you.

Getting Started Checklist

❑ Start your business plan

❑ Find training and mentors

❑ Subscribe to information sources to keep updated on your industry

❑ Find a small business lawyer you are comfortable with and trust

❑ With your lawyer, select your business structure:

    ○ Sole Proprietorship

    ○ Corporation

    ○ Partnership

    ○ Limited Liability Company

    ○ Other (some states have even more options!)

❑ With your accountant, determine your federal tax treatment (i.e., to be or not to be an S corporation).

What Would You Tell Your Best Friend About... GETTING STARTED

The most important insider secret that I would tell my best friend if she wanted to launch her own company would be to contact her local SCORE office. The retired business executives from SCORE have a lifetime of experience. They can help you with every aspect of business, from beginning to end. They have a wealth of educational materials, articles and contacts on their Web site, offer seminars and even one-to-one consulting.

Did I mention the advice from SCORE is free?

Mary Dawn Sullivan, Founder
Chair Flair
www.chairflairforyou.com

My advice would be: Don't do it alone. Success is a little bit about the product or service, but mostly a result of the team running the show. Find someone who is as passionate as you are, *but has a different skill set*. I've done it both ways and would never launch a company alone again. Plus, if you can't get someone excited enough to join you, perhaps it's not such a great business...

David Friedman, CEO
inhabi.com

Chapter 4:
Protect Your
Product Idea

In this chapter, we'll talk about how to protect your product idea and other intellectual property.

Patents

Inventors always want to patent their products. Notice I say "want." I didn't say "do" and I didn't say "should" because those are two very different things.

Let's start with what patents are and why you would want one.

A patent is a property right granted by the Government of the United States of America to an inventor "to exclude others from making, using, of-fering for sale, or selling the invention throughout the United States or importing the invention into the United States" for a limited time in exchange for public disclosure of the invention when the patent is granted. Source: uspto.gov

Two types of patents that we need to be concerned about here are the utility and design patents. Utility patents are just as their name implies: they protect how a product is used. Design patents have a pretty descriptive name, too: they protect how a product looks.

What you need to know is that while design patents may be easier to obtain, they don't offer the same protections as a utility patent. Think of it like this: I have this idea for a new dog brush that is connected to a foaming applicator and bottle. The top of the contraption is the dog brush and you pump it down to allow the foaming liquid to travel up from the bottle and out of the holes in the dog brush at the top. The idea is that you would combine two separate tools (i.e., a bottle of lotion/shampoo and a brush) for combing liquid onto your dog.

The product is unlikely to receive a utility patent because some-one holds a patent on the pumping applicator already (the way the product is used). If I applied for a design patent, I might be able to receive it for the shape of the brush and the bottle (the way that the contraption looks). However, if someone changed the shape of the brush head from round to square, for example, they might be able to produce the same type of product without infringing upon my design patent. My design patent wouldn't of-fer me the protection I was seeking.

So *do* inventors get patents? Yes, but the bottom line is they can be difficult to obtain. If you use a patent attorney, he or she can be expensive as well.

Now *should* you apply for a patent? Only you can provide that answer, but let's look at the pros and the cons. Patents can offer protection from someone copying your idea if it truly has a unique use or look. This could be a very lucrative thing, as you may be able to hold competition off for a good numbers of years (20 to be exact).

Another advantage of having a patent is that it is treated as an asset for your company. If you sell your company, a patent can provide a strong negotiating point for you in your company's valuation. Investors also like to see a company with a patent asset, as it makes their return on investment a little less risky. As investors see it, if you can protect your idea, you won't be facing as much direct competition and if your company fails, you can sell your patent, which will reap some value to return to the investors.

I wouldn't try to talk anyone out of getting a patent. There are things for you to consider, though. For example, the protection that a patent provides is only as good as the owner is willing and able to enforce it. Say that someone infringes upon your patent; it is up to you to find out that they've done it. No one is monitoring it for you. Then, it is up to you to politely ask them to stop, or to hire a lawyer to write a letter and politely ask them to stop. If it goes further, you may have to pay your lawyer to bring a case against the infringer and fund a potentially expensive and drawn-out legal process.

If you decide you do want to pursue a patent, you'll need to submit a patent application to the US Patent & Trademark Office.

It is possible for you to submit it yourself, but patent language is pretty much like a foreign language. You'll probably want to invest the dollars to hire a patent attorney. If you do decide to fly solo on this, you can submit your patent application with forms available on www.uspto.gov.

Provisional Patent Application

Every time I say something about "a provisional patent" my lawyer patiently reminds me that there is no such thing. The Provisional Patent *Application,* however, is a document that you file with the USPTO, which acts like a placeholder. It keeps your place in line by establishing an early filing date for your patent so you can file a Non-Provisional Patent Application later. The provisional application only lasts one year, so at the end of the year, you need to file for the full patent or re-file an application to keep your place in line.

The best thing about a Provisional Patent Application is that you get to keep working on your product idea and Non-Provisional Patent Application while it holds that place for you. And you get to write "patent pending" on your packaging!

Because it is cheaper than filing for a Non-Provisional Patent, many small businesses who decide to license their products, opt for a Provisional Patent Application. This allows them to work on getting a licensee while maintaining some protection over their idea. Additionally, once a licensee signs on, the licensee may have more resources to pay for the Non-Provisional Patent Application.

Trademarks

While obtaining a patent can be an arduous and often unrewarding process, trademarks are much easier to obtain, and they too can become very valuable assets for your company.

What is a trademark?

> *A trademark is a word, phrase, symbol or design, or a combination thereof, that identifies and distinguishes the source of the goods of one party from those of others.* Source: uspto.gov

Like a patent, a trademark is intellectual property. You can think of intellectual property as simply something made by your brain. Because you made it, or hired someone to make it for you, it belongs to you. And the government grants you, and you alone, the right to use that property.

With your unique company name and/or your product name, you can start building your brand. When someone sees your product's name or logo, they start to form mental impressions about what they know about it. Think of any brand name that you know; you immediately start to think of attributes associated with that brand. For example, think of Volvo. What was the first word that popped into your head? Volvo hopes your answer is: safety. The Volvo-brand team has worked very hard and very long for that to happen. If they hadn't protected their name, any company could have started using it. Imagine the brand confusion if a discount car company also were able to use the Volvo name.

So, you should register your company name and your product name with the US Patent and Trademark Office. With the limited budgets usually associated with startups, the next question often is, should I register my name, or my logo, or both? Because we're talking about products, we'll talk about your product name for now, but some of the same challenges apply with your company name as well.

If you have the money, you should register both the product name and your product logo. If you are strapped for cash, as so many new entrepreneurs are, and can only afford to register one, the prevailing wisdom is that you should register your product name without restrictions. This means that you should register just the name without specifying any font, color, or characters. Typically, this will keep other businesses from using your name. They may however be able to use elements of your logo.

If you do decide to apply for a trademark, begin using the ™ symbol with your name and/or logo. It is an unregistered trademark that says that your mark is "in use." It does offer some protection in certain cases, but does not afford you the same protection as when your trademark becomes registered, which is signified as ®. Keep track of when you first started using the name and/or logo commercially as that is one of the things the US PTO will need to know when you apply.

The trademark paperwork at uspto.gov is relatively easy to do yourself. If you are not comfortable with it, you can hire an intellectual property attorney to do it for you, or work with companies like LegalZoom.com, that often charge you a small fee in addition to the filing fees.

What Would You Tell Your Best Friend About... COMMITMENT?

I would try to talk them out of it. HARD. The TIME, $$, Stress, and you will be a boring person constantly and only working on the business. This is a backwards way of judging their commitment and passion. You have to have screws missing (not just loose) and you have to be so hard-headed to survive.

Brad Barrett, Founder, President
GrillGrate, LLC
www.grillgrate.com

The journey from taking an idea to fruition can be one of the most difficult yet exciting experiences of your life. A key thing to remember in bringing your product idea to the marketplace is to always do your homework—whether it's researching your patent attorney or determining the appropriate retail buyers for your product. It only takes one original idea to become an entrepreneur, and using the countless resources available to you will only help to make that thought a reality. Just do it!

Kendall Thompson, Founder and Creator
Kenmark Sports, LLC
www.kenmarksports.com

Chapter 5:
Making Your Product

If you've done your prep work and decided you want to take your product all the way to the marketplace, you're in the right place. And, if you've decided you're an idea person or a licensor and don't want to run a business or manufacture your product, stay along for the ride. You may just decide the process is more exciting—and easier—than you first thought!

There are many important steps before you can begin the process of manufacturing your product. One of those steps is determining how you are going to pay for your prototype (if needed) and your first production run. It's hard to know how much money you'll need, though, until you start asking the right questions of the right people.

To get your product made, you may need some or all of the following people and tools, all of which are described in detail further below:

- A prototype to bring to potential customers and retail buyers

- Design professionals to help develop your prototype

- A manufacturer to build your product

- If you're manufacturing overseas, a sourcing agent to act as a go-between for you and your overseas manufacturer

- If you're manufacturing overseas, a customs broker to bring your product into the US

- A packaging company to package your product

- A warehouse to store your product.

We'll get into marketing, fulfillment, and channels of distribution in later chapters.

Prototype

This is where the fun begins! The prototype stage of the product launch is where you finally begin to see your idea take shape.

If a picture is worth a thousand words, a prototype is worth a million. Instead of waving your hands around the air and trying to get someone to visualize your idea, now you can wave your hands around the prototype.

One objective of the prototype is to refine your idea before you manufacture any products. You may decide to take it to a trade-show and show potential consumers or retailers for their feedback. You may use it in a real environment to see if your design holds up to actual conditions. However you test it, this is the stage to get the kinks out.

Depending on your product and the purpose of your test, you may choose an informal or formal prototype. For simple tests or to show at a focus group, your prototype can be as informal as another product that you manipulated to show how your product would work.

If you're showing actual customers or pre-selling retailers or dis-tributors, you may need your prototype produced with more formal finishes. The good news is that new technology has made getting a professional-looking prototype easier, cheaper, and less time-intensive. Your next step is to get in touch with a profes-sional prototyping firm or fabric manufacturer.

The Professionals

Professional prototypes can be very powerful tools, even before you manufacture your first product. A friend of mine used a pro-fessional prototype to sell her yet-to-be-manufactured products to retail buyers at a tradeshow. She even ended up making a sale to a major department store chain!

For plastics and other solid materials, either your manufacturer or a professional prototyping firm can help you develop the prototype. These are the steps your idea will likely go through on its way to becoming a prototype:

A Really Fancy Drawing

A product design engineer or other professional will meet with you to hear your idea. After several discussions, he or she will use a Computer-Aided Design (CAD) software program to turn the idea in your head into a dimensional drawing.

Your Product Goes Virtual!

From there, your dimensional drawing may go to a virtual prototyping stage, where your product can be tested and evaluated using simulation software. This software will run your virtual product through various tests to determine the best way to design it for optimal performance. This stage between the CAD drawing and the actual physical prototype can save you and your manufacturers hundreds, if not thousands, of dollars and a significant amount of time. This stage catches many design flaws and fixes them before you go to the next step.

Let's Get Physical

Sometimes, you can explain or even sell your ideas right from the virtual prototyping stage. If you need a physical representation though, your product will likely go through rapid prototyping. At this stage, using the output from the CAD drawing and/or the virtual prototyping stages, a large tooling machine will build your prototype in layers. The rapid prototyping process likely will cost you only a few hundred dollars, plus the fees from the prototyping firm, if you use one.

If you need a highly accurate prototype though, your product may go through a Rapid Injection Molding process. It is not as time consuming and costly as older processes, such as injection molding or machining, and it delivers a more accurate prototype than the rapid prototyping process.

For fabric prototypes, with a little bit of information like the type of fabric you want, the desired colors, size range, and packaging requirements, there are many fabric manufacturers who will create a sample for you, typically for under $500.00. If you have crafted your own sample to share with your fabric manufacturer, all the better—the fabric manufacture can often suggest fabric types and work with you on patterns and sizes.

Both the prototyping firms and the fabric manufacturers may offer you suggestions on the materials you should use. If they don't, ask. You may think rubber is the right material when it turns out that PVC plastic is a better solution for your specific product. If you don't ask, you won't know.

You can find professional prototyping firms and fabric manufacturers at www.ThomasNet.com. Type in either "rapid prototyping services" or "fabric" into the product/service box.

If you do not want to go with a firm or company but would rather work one-on-one with a product engineer or a seamstress, choose a freelance provider Web site like elance.com or guru.com. Typically these professionals will work on a project basis or a limited hourly basis. Their designs may be enough to bring to your manufacturer and you may be able to skip the prototype stage altogether.

Insider secret: While you're designing your prototype, you need to consider how much the actual production is going to cost. Be sure that whoever works with you on your prototype or CAD drawing keeps the end cost of manufacturing in mind. The last thing you want is to have a great prototype that would cost too much to produce in the real world. Additionally, start thinking about your product packaging at this stage. Read further in this chapter for a money- and time-saving tip.

Working with US Manufacturers

Depending on your product, you may have many options when it comes to manufacturers for your product or you may have only a few.

For me, the first step was to look for manufacturers in the US. The advantages of using a US manufacturer often include the capability of doing smaller production runs and typically net 30 days to pay your invoices.

The leading source for finding US and Canadian manufacturers is ThomasNet.com, though there are a variety of other sources. On ThomasNet.com, you can filter the manufacturers by location, product type, and type (e.g., custom manufacturer, distributor, etc.).

When you first contact your manufacturer, they will want to see your prototype or CAD drawing, unless they already produce a product similar to yours. They'll want to know your initial run quantities and time frames.

For your part, you should ask manufacturers to give you a formal quote with:

- Prices for at least 3 different quantities. Don't be afraid to tell them a very low quantity to start with. It's best to know what they will charge you for a small production run rather than assuming that they'll charge you the same price per unit for 100 units as they quoted you for 1,000 units

- Their lead time, i.e., how long will it take to get your product? And, if they do not deliver in that time frame, will they accept a late charge?

Though manufacturers typically want net 30 days, sometimes you can negotiate your payment terms as net 45 days or net 60 days; these are how many days you have to pay them after receipt of their invoice. Also, ask them upfront what their return policy is for damaged product or product that doesn't meet your quality requirements. Get the quote and all of the policy information in writing. And if you change your quantity, have your manufacturer send you a revised quote in writing with the new costs.

If you have several options for manufacturers, make sure you ask at least two or three of them to provide you with quotes. If the prices are comparable, work with the manufacturer you have the most rapport with, but be sure to keep the numbers of the other ones handy. Despite how well it works out in the beginning, nearly every entrepreneur I've spoken with has had at least one really bad experience with a manufacturer. Most, including me, had to get a new manufacturer very quickly and already having other manufacturers waiting in the wings was crucial.

Working with Overseas Manufacturers

There are going to be times and instances where you may need or want to work with overseas manufacturers. For instance, there may be no one in the US who manufactures what you need. You may find that US manufacturers are unwilling to retool their machines for your specific sizes, your unique product, or the size of your production run.

Some current trends are impacting long-held beliefs about the advantages and pitfalls to working with non-US companies. Wages in Asia are rising so production costs are becoming a little less attractive. Perhaps to counter the rising labor costs, some Asian manufacturers are offering shorter production runs. Where once you needed to purchase in the hundreds of thousands of units, some manufacturers in China are offering production runs as low as 500-1,000 units, depending on the product.

Though the actual production times are comparable, the lead times to receive products from overseas is still typically 2-3 months, versus only weeks with a US manufacturer. From payment receipt, to ship freight times, to custom clearance, everything seems to take at least a week longer than you expect.

Payment terms are also different working with an overseas vendor. I usually want to inspect my products before I send in the payment but you don't get that option with overseas manufacturers.

Payment to overseas companies is nearly always expected up-front and is typically made through a wire transfer. That's a hard concept for small business owners who can pay Net 30 with US vendors. Once the overseas manufacturers get to know and trust you, though, the payment terms can become more favorable.

Also, the exchange rate fluctuations may impact your costs. Be sure to ask for a quote very close to your order date, or have the manufacturer specify for how long the quote is valid.

If you're purchasing an existing product, there are sites like Alibaba. com and others that pre-qualify some overseas manufacturers and their products. However, if you have to work directly with the overseas manufacturer to produce prototypes or products, you may want to work with a sourcing agent. These go-betweens are typically fluent in the language of the manufacturer and can help you communicate your needs most effectively. They also have net-works of manufacturers that they work with and can help you find the most trustworthy companies. If you choose a good one, the sourcing agent can help you problem solve and come up with ideas as well.

Once your product is made, there are two ways for your products to come into the US, by ship or by air. Air is very expensive, un-less you have a small quantity of lightweight products. So, it is likely that your products will come by boat. There are a number of ports for the products to come into the US. Typically, for prod-ucts manufactured in Asia, the ports used are Los Angeles or San Francisco, but there are ports all over the US coasts.

Your overseas manufacturer typically arranges the shipment to the US port via a freight forwarder (a shipper) and charges you the freight fee, which will depend on which port you choose. Ask your freight forwarder or your manufacturer for the costs and time frames for various ports before you decide. You may find using a port on the East Coast is cheaper than having your product come into Los Angeles and then ground transported to you in Atlanta, for example.

If your manufacturer does not arrange the freight forwarder for you, you can search on the Internet for an international shipping company or choose one of the big guys, like UPS Ocean Freight or Old Dominion. Whichever one you select, be sure it ships from your manufacturer's location to the US, preferably to the port you've chosen.

The shipping company can arrange for your product to be picked up from your manufacturer and brought to the manufacturer's country port. It will then go on the boat headed to the US. Once it arrives, a customs services agent will take over. A custom services agent is someone you hire to handle the customs process for you with the US Customs Department.

You will need to provide important documents to the customs services agent, including: the invoice from your manufacturer, a list of the goods included in the shipment, the weight and size of the shipment, and proof of origin.

Be sure to give very accurate information to your customs services agents as the US Customs Department can get a little cranky if the documents aren't 100% correct. A cranky US Customs Department could mean fines and other headaches for you.

Attention-Getting Packaging

Just like the cover of a book, your product packaging is designed to get attention. Quickly. A merchandise representative from CVS told me that, in his store, products have less than 4 seconds to grab a consumer's attention. So in 4 seconds or less, the packaging needs to tell your product's story and appeal to your target audience on an emotional level.

That's a tall order for paper, cardboard, plastic, or cellophane.

Design professionals have been challenged by this for a number of years. A good designer with product experience in your industry could become your best friend.

The time to think about packaging is as early as when you're working on your prototype. That's because packaging can be a very costly portion of your Cost of Goods Sold (COGS) if you don't think it through carefully up front. (If you don't know what COGS is yet, don't worry; Chapter 7 breaks it all down for you).

Before we get to the different types of packaging, you need to ask yourself, "How am I going to sell my product?" Are you going to sell it online or through retailers? Are you going to drop-ship for wholesale vendors? If you don't know at this point, that's okay. The next chapter will discuss your various options. But keep in mind that where you sell will have an impact on your packaging.

If you sell on the Internet, your product will likely need to be packed in a box or envelope and shipped. When you're at the prototype stage, consider this carefully. Say you're creating a brand new designer frying pan. Instead of the ordinary black non-stick coating, you've used your artist background to design it with a masterpiece-like picture on the cooking surface. The handle is just an ordinary handle that you don't put much thought into. What happens if that handle is one inch too long for standard-box packaging? To make your frying pan fit into the packaging, you'll need to go up one standard box size, which leaves a lot of room, and so now you need protective packaging material. So you opt for a customized box. Very costly.

What if instead, at the prototype stage, you thought about the product packaging? You and your prototyping firm tested your prototype out with a few boxes and then shortened your handle to fit in the standard box. You have just saved a lot of money!

Early on, you may be able to do the packaging yourself. If it's a beautiful product itself, your packaging can be very simple. Consider just a product label or a header card if it is going into retail stores. You can also get various sizes of polybags from supply vendors like Uline.com and other suppliers to create some inexpensive, professional-looking packaging.

If you find packaging your product yourself is time consuming, or not as attractive as you would prefer, contact a packaging company in your area. You may be surprised that the costs are not as high as you first imagined—especially if you thought through your packaging at the prototype stage! Some of the packaging companies will warehouse your product for a monthly fee and some offer ecommerce-fulfillment solutions.

UPC Barcodes

If you sell your product through retailers or via the Internet from anywhere other than your own site, you're most likely going to need a Universal Product Code (UPC) barcode. Manufacturers and retailers use UPC barcodes to track products throughout the supply chain.

You may have just called them barcodes because of the black horizontal lines, but their proper name is UPC barcode. That's because they also include numbers underneath the bars that also identify the manufacturer, the product category, and the product SKU.

UPC barcodes are so critical to a retailer's supply chain efficiency that some of the larger retailers will tell you exactly how big your UPC barcode image can be and where it needs to be placed on your packaging. If you think you don't need one because you're selling online, you may not be correct. Amazon.com requires UPC barcodes and other large online retailers are following suit.

The official UPC barcode agency is GS1 US (www.gs1us.org). The US UPC barcodes follow GS1's standards. For approximately $760.00 you can get 100 UPC barcodes for one year. Don't need 100? Well, GS1 doesn't sell them in units less than 100. If you're tempted to buy only a few UPC barcodes from a barcodes broker, you should reconsider it.

Recall that I said the numbers under the vertical bars identify the manufacturer? That's because they include a prefix that is unique to the company that buys the UPC barcode. Each code includes the prefix. What happens is that some companies buy the 100 codes from GS1 and start selling them off individually or a few at a time to smaller companies with fewer products. The problem is that the prefix identifies the original purchaser of the codes from GS1. For retailers, this can present significant challenges and headaches within their supply chain. As such, many retailers will not accept UPC barcodes for which you are not the original purchaser. If you want to work with them, you will need to buy the codes from GS1 anyway. You're better off just starting with the official organization. And, while the initial fee is approximately $760, the renewal fees are usually around $150 annually.

Your individual product and a case of your product, which is typically 10-12 units, usually will have different UPC barcodes.

Where Will You Store It?

Once your product is packaged, you need a place to store your inventory. How and where you are going to sell your product will impact your decision here. The next chapter will go into the channels of distribution further, but general warehousing options include the following:

- If you are going to mail the product yourself, then you may want to have the inventory shipped to your home. If you have a significant amount of inventory, your packaging company may be able to store the bulk of your inventory for you for a small monthly fee.

- If you are going to have a fulfillment center mail your product for you, they will have a warehouse and the storage cost is typically included in their overall fees.

- If you are working with a distributor, they often have warehouses to store your product and may do so for a fee or may work it into the price they pay you for your product.

- If you are working with a retailer(s) directly and they have given you an order, you may be able to ship your product directly to them. Note that some retailers use Electronic Data Interchange (EDI) to manage their inventory and supply chain. If you are shipping directly from your packaging company, make sure your packaging company knows the retailer's requirements for EDI and labeling of boxes.

Mailing Tips

If you are going to warehouse products at your own home and sell your product via your Web site or drop-ship it for a larger vendor, you need to take some time to learn about mailing your specific product.

Once you have your Web site up and running (see Chapter 6 for more information on ecommerce Web sites), you may be able to link your shopping cart into the Web sites of UPS, FedEx, USPS, and others. This will provide dynamic shipping costs based on the products your customer chooses and her or his mailing address.

You may, however, need or want to put a fixed shipping price on your product to cover the costs of shipping. To determine how much your product weighs, go on to a shipping site to determine the cost for shipping the product the farthest distance from you. Add in extra fees for any handling costs you may have, like a fulfillment company's fee. Also, determine what the shippers' extra fees are for shipping to Alaska and Hawaii. If applicable, add those fees in for customers ordering from those states.

Plug these numbers into the mailing specification in your Web site's shopping cart, or have your Web site guru do it for you.

If your product fits into the standard-size mailing boxes of the United States Postal Service or FedEx, then you won't have to pay for shipping boxes. That's a cost savings for you, and again, one to consider at the prototype stage. If you ship with UPS or need to provide your own boxes, you can find a number of box vendors online.

Insider secret: If your product is large but lightweight, the major shipping vendors may charge you based on dimensional weight versus actual weight. It could be a big cost for you, so it's worth explaining. Shipping trucks are filled based on weight not based on the number of boxes. This is why, typically, the shipping company charges you by the weight of your box. The heavier it is, the more you pay. However, if you were selling an extra-large teddy bear, for example, your box would be very large but it wouldn't weigh as much as, say, a similarly sized box of books. Because your teddy bear box would take up a lot space but wouldn't normally bring in as much money, the shipping company may measure your box by dimensional weight, i.e., what your box would typically weigh if it were filled with something other than a lightweight teddy bear.

Check your shipping vendor's requirements and how they measure dimensional weight before you decide to sell that great big teddy bear online.

Making Your Product Checklist

- ❑ Determine if, to sell your idea, you need a prototype or a CAD drawing to show to potential customers and retail buyers

- ❑ If you need a prototype, determine whether you need the help of a professional prototyping-services firm

- ❑ Keep packaging and mailing in mind as you develop your prototype

- ❑ Identify potential manufacturers

- ❑ Ask 2–3 manufacturers to quote on your project

- ❑ If you're manufacturing overseas, find a sourcing agent to act as a go-between for you and your overseas manufacturer

- ❑ If you're manufacturing overseas, find a customs services agent to help bring your product into the US

- ❑ Identify packaging companies to package your product

- ❑ Ask 2–3 packaging companies to quote on your project

- ❑ Identify a warehouse to store your product, if necessary.

What Would You Tell Your Best Friend About... MANUFACTURING?

I would give the following advice to my friend who wanted to launch a product: definitely do it—but only after thorough research to ensure a similar version is not already out there and/or patented and that there is market demand. Once you've got that under your belt, I would recommend you manufacture it vs. license it. The world is your oyster if you have control of the manufacturing, and thus the marketing and distribution, of your own product. The profits are far greater as well.

Michal Chesal, President
Baby K'tan, LLC
www.babyktan.com

My advice would be to keep tight control of the process. I was headed down the road where a friend who is in the business was going to have his manufacturer create my product. But, I never had the option of speaking directly with them, and unfortunately I wasted 6 precious months.

Aly Benson, Founder
Whippy Clip
www.whippyclip.com

Chapter 6:
How Are You Going to Sell It?

A channel of distribution is just a fancy way of describing how you are going to get your product to your customer. In other words, how are you going to sell and deliver products? For selling your product, you have a lot of options, including:

- Online

- Through Retailers: specialty, big box, department, drug stores, grocery stores, etc.

- Through Distributors

- Via Drop-Shipping

- Direct

Which option(s) you choose will have an impact on your marketing, your pricing, your packaging, and ultimately your profit.

Your Own Site

If you choose to sell your product online, you're in good company. According to Forrester Research, ecommerce is growing at double-digit rates each year and is expected to grow to $335 billion this year. Given the growth rates, more ecommerce solutions companies are jumping into the industry to help aspiring entrepreneurs get their online stores up and running.

Given how many options are available to you, it can be difficult to know what to do. Should you build your own site or have someone do it for you? Should you go with a vendor who offers a full Web site package?

If you can afford it, my recommendation is to choose a vendor who basically provides an ecommerce store in a box (or at least a virtual box). These comprehensive solutions can set you up with a Web site template or customized site, a monthly hosting service, a shopping cart, and even access to a merchant account. Besides having all of the elements you need in one solution, the user interface with these solutions is usually so easy that you can quickly update your Web site content, prices, packaging, inventory, and more by yourself.

The ecommerce store vendor will charge you a monthly hosting fee typically based on the number of products you sell. Volusion, for example, offers monthly packages ranging from $19.00 a month for up to 100 products to $149.00 for an unlimited number of products.

If you decide to develop the Web site yourself or with a designer, you should have at least the following pages:

- Home Page
- About Page
- Product Page
- Order Page
- Contact Page

You or your designer should also include a shopping cart. There are so many good shopping cart plug-ins that there is no need for you to redesign the wheel.

Once your shopping cart is set up, you will need a payment service to enable your online store to process credit card payments. You may choose to link your shopping cart to PayPal, to a merchant account service, or to both.

PayPal will charge you a percentage fee, plus a small fixed fee based on the cost of the sale. For monthly sales of up to $3,000, the fees are 2.9% of the sale plus 30 cents. The percentages go down as the monthly sales go up.

Merchant accounts will charge you similar percentage fees but they also typically have a monthly fee. You can shop around to get the best fees.

The advantage of selling from your own Web site is that you get to keep more of the gross revenue from your sales. The disadvantage is that you have to draw people to your site and that can sometimes be a costly proposition. And once potential customers are on your site, you have to convince them to buy. One other disadvantage is that you have to pay a monthly hosting fee for your Web site. It's usually $25-$35 but you have to pay that fee each month whether you make any sales or not.

Drop-Shipping for Other Stores

It's becoming more commonplace for online sites of all kinds and sizes to add drop-shipped products to their Web sites to fill out their product lines. Drop-shipping is when the owner of the site takes no ownership of your inventory, but sells it to their customers, typically online or through a catalog. Once the order is submitted by the customer, the site owner sends the order to you for shipment.

Typically with drop-shipping for larger retailers, you're not allowed to include any of your own promotional material in the package. Often, the retailer will send you a packing slip with the company logo and information to include in the package. So, as far as the end customer knows the product came from the other company's store.

It used to be that drop-shippers only took 20% of your retail price. So again, if your product sold for $19.99, they'd charge you $4 for selling your product to their customer. Now, as bigger retailers get into the game, some are still expecting wholesale prices, meaning they take 50% of your retail price, or $10.

From an entrepreneur's perspective, the problem is that in the offline world, when you sell to a retailer at the very special wholesale price, you no longer have anything to do with that inventory. The retailer owns it, does the sale and customer service, and if necessary the shipping. With drop-shipping, you're still on the hook for shipping and sometimes, even the customer service.

When large retailers have asked me to drop-ship at wholesale prices, I have pushed back a few times with some modest success. It is an interesting area to watch to see how savvy entrepreneurs deal with this.

Traditional Retailers

Retailers are great because they give you access to so many customers that you wouldn't likely be able to reach on your own. Retailers are not so great because they want a big chunk of your profits. There are a few different types of retailers, but they typically want different sizes of margins, so it's worth looking at a few of them.

Smaller Specialty Retailers

Specialty retailers are small- to medium-sized, brick-and-mortar retail stores. Many are owned by families or by individuals as opposed to corporations. Depending on your industry, these retailers will likely want "keystone pricing." Keystone is a pricing method of simply doubling the wholesale price to determine the retail price. For you, the small business owner, that means the retailer wants to buy your product at half of the retail price. So if your product sells at $19.99, the specialty retailer wants to buy it from you for $10.00 (i.e., the wholesale price).

Big Box and Other Large Retailers

Run by corporations, Big Box Stores are the mega-chain stores like Target, Best Buy, and Wal-Mart. Depending on the chain, the margins can be razor thin when working with these behemoths. But no one can deliver the number of customers who will potentially buy your product like the big guys.

Working with Big Box Retailers is difficult for most small companies. The retailer often wants enough product inventory to stock each of their stores. Additionally, they require their vendors to work with robust inventory systems. All of this can be overwhelming to a small company with limited resources and big dreams.

Sometimes the Big Box Retailers will offer a test to new vendors. Most often, this means rolling out your product to their stores in one region. If the product does well in that region, they may roll the product out to other regions. This could help smaller companies deal with inventory ramp ups. But working with a Big Box Retailer right off the bat is not always an ideal situation for a small company.

Other large retailers, like Home Depot and Petsmart, can be easier for small companies to work with as they have fewer stores and are able to be more flexible in their processing.

Department Stores

Facing a lot of competition from both online and brick-and-mortar stores, department stores vary greatly on their margin requirements. Some even have different requirements based on the category of product within their own stores. Often, department stores will mark up your wholesale price by 60-65%.

That means that, if your wholesale price to all retailers is, for example, $10, the department store may mark up your price to only $16-16.50. Recall that with keystone pricing, the specialty retailer doubles your wholesale price, means they're selling it for $20.00. You're still getting the same $10.00 from the specialty retailer and the department store, so why should you care about the price at which either sells your product?

Actually, you should care very much. Retailers do not like to compete with each other on price and you will not win any friends, or repeat business, if you inadvertently allow retailers to undercut each other. However, once you sell your product to a retailer, you cannot often specify the ultimate retail price. Knowing this, you may want to research the store you're negotiating with to see if you can determine their typical mark up. In our above situation, you may want to offer the department store a wholesale price of $12-12.50. The higher wholesale price and smaller markup may even things out for all of your retail customers.

Chain Drug Stores

I have met several small businesses that have had success with reaching out to the pharmacy and chain drug stores to carry their products. Walgreens, in particular, allows their store managers to make product decisions. You can typically pitch your product directly to the store manager in your area. If your product makes it into a local store or multiple local stores, your store manager(s) may pitch to the regional store manager and on up to the national level.

In contrast, CVS makes product decisions at the corporate level. On rare occasions, they will do a test, but typically, if they accept your product, they will roll it out to 7,000+ stores at one time.

Insider secret: Drug stores do take products that retail at higher prices but they prefer lower-priced items as customers will impulse-buy more products that are under $10.

Reaching Out to Retailers

The average retailer does not make products. Therefore, they need products from companies to stock their shelves and sell to their customers. That means that they need someone just like you. So, reach out to them and ask them to carry your product. The worst thing that can happen is that they say "No."

To begin your sales efforts, make a list of the retailers who carry similar products as yours. You may think you know which retailers you need to reach out to, but do a little research anyway. Many stores are expanding their product offerings and including items they don't traditionally carry to appeal to a bigger customer base. Consider hardware stores and groceries. Also, consider drug and pharmacy stores that carry a diverse set of products and are eager to be seen as convenient and innovative by their customers.

Once you have your list, begin with their Web sites. Large retailers often have specific processes for you to follow to begin your vendor discussions. Most will include their vendor guidelines right on their site to outline their preferred approach. These guidelines will tell you how to submit your product or whom to reach out to within their company.

If you are working with smaller retailers or cannot find the vendor guidelines, use LinkedIn to find the retailer's purchasing director, merchandising director, or senior buyer. The title usually depends on the size of the retailer. Some retailers even break out their buyers' titles by category, e.g., Women's Accessories Buyer.

Using the Internet, see if you can find your contacts' email addresses. If not, see if you can find anyone at the company's email address and use the same syntax for your contact(s).

In your email, describe your product and include why it would be beneficial for your retailer to carry the product. Remember, you are speaking to the *retailer* not the end-customer. He or she is not going to *use* your product; they are going to *sell* it. The benefits to a retailer are different than the benefits for an end customer. When you speak to a retailer, you need to use terms like profits and favorable margins.

After you send your email, follow up with a phone call a week later. Yes, you're going to have to do more than reach out via email. They can ignore your email, but a phone call is more insistent. You'll likely get your contact's voice mail, so leave a message. In your message say that you're following up to set up time to speak with him or her and that you will call back in a few days. Then follow up immediately with an email with the same information. That way the retailer can listen to your voice mail and respond via email.

When you get your first meeting with the retailer, be sure to remember that you're selling profits and margins. Also, tell him or her about your marketing efforts. Even though he or she will be selling the product, you need to compel the customers to buy it with advertising and promotional efforts. (See Chapter 8 for more on that subject).

It may take a few attempts to land a meeting with a retailer, but keep trying. If one says no, there are always more stores in the strip mall! Keep trying. Once you land one retailer, you can use that success to reach out to others.

For more information on reaching out to and closing retailers, contact one of the many coaches and mentors that specialize in this. As one of many resources available to you, consider Kim Lavine's, of Mommy Millionaire, course on Breaking Down the Doors to Big Retail. Note that men do take that course, too!

Distributors

Distributors are companies that have established relationships with retailers, often specialty retailers. Their sales people meet with retailers often and share new products and pricing promotions. The advantage of working with distributors is that they typically have a much bigger reach than you do. Sure, you could visit every small retailer in your category in a 60-mile radius, but it would take an extraordinary amount of time—to set up the meetings, to drive to the locations, and make the sales. Then, you would have to deliver the product, manage the customer service, and follow up for additional sales.

The distributor takes much of that work off your hands. For a price. Typically distributors want to make 35-40% on your product. And keep in mind, their customer is the same as yours: the specialty retailer who wants keystone pricing no matter whom they buy your product from. So, if your wholesale price is $10, the distributor will want to buy the product from you at $7-7.50. Then, they'll turn around and sell it to the retailer at $10.00.

One important note about distributors and retailers: even if you're going to be merchandising your product through distributors or retailers, you *still have to sell your product*. That means that distributors and retailers can get your product onto retail shelves and in front of potential customers, but you are still going to have to do the promotions and activities to pique the interest of the customer and get them to buy.

Direct Response

Switching from brick-and-mortar to television brings us to direct response selling via infomercials. Infomercials are ½-hour long commercials that sell directly from the TV to the customer via a 1-800 number or Web site. In the past, these direct response television commercials were cost-prohibitive to small companies; to the tune of $20,000 and up. Now, however, savvy marketing folks have created short-form infomercials. These shorter infomercials last for a few minutes to several minutes and are much more affordable for small companies.

Advertising agencies specializing in TV commercials can create short-form infomercials for as low as $5,000. Keep in mind, that amount typically doesn't include the air-time charges.

The "As Seen on TV" folks have embraced short-form infomercials with a vengeance and are working hard to get the products of smaller companies on television. Be careful though, they also are skimming nearly all of the profit to get their customers' products in front of large TV audiences!

*Business plan alert: the distribution channel(s) you choose will have a direct impact on your business plan and should be included in the sales and marketing section!

What Would You Tell Your Best Friend About… SALES?

As a solo entrepreneur, I have a successful startup (i.e., profitable) with a very well-received product and I still tell anyone who wants to listen to stay out of entrepreneurship!!! I was in corporate marketing for almost 30 years, but had absolutely no idea what I was getting into when I started this business. Also, I did not realize that 80% of having a successful business is sales-related..........and I hate sales.

Jo Anne Patterson
The Shoul
www.theshoul.com

I would tell my best friend to focus your time on selling and not the product. Get the product "good enough" and you can make adjustments later. Most people expect a "good enough" product from a startup. You can be very busy fixing and perfecting your product, but that will never bring in a single sale.

Daniel Alarik
Founder, Owner, Drill Sargent
Grunt Style LLC
www.gruntstyle.com

Chapter 7:
How Are You Going to Pay for It?

Thinking about how to pay for the production and marketing of your product is probably keeping you up at night. But you can't really know how you're going to pay for something until you know how much it's going to cost.

Enter your financial documents.

Financials

Don't let the financial aspect of your business terrify you. Even if you can't balance a budget, you can do this. That's because there are only three things you really need to know (or estimate) right now:

1. Your potential sales
2. Your costs to make, package, and sell your products
3. Your everyday expenses

Knowing these three things can do many important things for you:

- Clarify your sales goals
- Forecast your income and costs
- Assess your progress against your sales goals
- Track your profits and losses
- Compare the performance of your channels of distribution
- Estimate the amount needed to run your business

Your Sales (Gross Revenues)

Your sales are called gross revenues because none of your costs for making and selling your product have been taken out yet.

The money you make per unit of product is going to be different for each channel of distribution. So, let's stay with the easy example from earlier and say that your product sells for $20. (Which, of course, you would really price at $19.99 or even $19.97, but round numbers are easier to calculate!). For this example, we'll assume you're selling online on your own Web site and through a specialty retailer.

- Your online gross revenue is likely to be $20 per unit because the total retail price is being paid to you by the customer

- The revenue per unit from your specialty retailer is likely to be $10 because you'll sell it to your retailer at the wholesale price of $10, and they'll turn around and sell it to the customer for $20

Now, how many products do you think you can sell each month? Even if you don't have the foggiest idea, take a guess and start playing with the numbers. Choose a really conservative number like 10. Then choose a really high number like 1,000. Think about whether you can realistically produce and sell 1,000 units every month. Maybe 1,000 units a month isn't what you can do right now; maybe 25, 50, or 100 is realistic. Find a number that starts to make sense from production costs and sales perspectives.

Now, do the same exercise with what you think your retailer will buy from you each month. Keep in mind that your retailer is going to buy by cases, not individual units. So, if your case size is 10 units, think about how many cases they will buy. Is 10 cases realistic? If so, that's 100 units a month.

It's okay if you don't know what is really doable at this point. This is just an exercise to get you to start grounding your thinking into actual numbers.

Once you have somewhat realistic numbers, multiply them by your revenue per unit discussed in the bullet points above.

You can start plugging your numbers into the table below. If you're savvy with Excel or another spreadsheet program, put this into a worksheet. If you're not comfortable with Excel, you can create the sales forecast on paper first, and then work your way up to working with a spreadsheet.

GROSS SALES FORECAST

Months

	1	2	3	4	5	6	7	8	9	10	11	12	Total
Revenues by Channel													
Internet													
Retail													
Total Revenues													

For our example, we'll use 25 units that you'll sell online and your retailer will buy 10 cases (i.e., 10 cases of 10 units each = 100 units) from you each month.

- Online: 25 units x $20 gross revenue = $500

- Retail: 100 units x $10 gross revenue = $1000

- Total per month* = $1500

GROSS SALES FORECAST

							Months						
	1	2	3	4	5	6	7	8	9	10	11	12	Total
Revenues by Channel													
Internet	$500	$500	$500	$500	$500	$500	$500	$500	$500	$500	$500	$500	$6000
Retail	$1000	$1000	$1000	$1000	$1000	$1000	$1000	$1000	$1000	$1000	$1000	$1000	$12000
Total Revenues	$1500	$1500	$1500	$1500	$1500	$1500	$1500	$1500	$1500	$1500	$1500	$1500	$18000

*When you actually record your gross revenues, they will fluctuate each month based on your sales. For example purposes, we are estimating them to be the same each month.

You've just created your sales forecast!

Your Product Costs (Cost of Goods Sold)

Your Cost of Goods Sold (COGS) is just what the phrase sounds like. It's how much it costs you to make, package, and ship your product to the place where it will be sold. From your manufacturer's quote, you have an estimate of what it will cost to make your product. The manufacturer should also give you a freight estimate, which is the cost to get your product from the manufacturer to its next destination; e.g., you, your packaging company, or other location where you will prepare your product for being sold.

Note that if your manufacturer hasn't broken out the cost by unit, add up all of the costs and the freight and divide it by the number of product units you are ordering.

For our example, let's assume these per unit costs are from your manufacturing quote:

- Product: $2.95
- Freight: $0.55
- Total Manufacturing Costs = $3.50

If you're working with a packaging company, they also have given you a quote on how much it will cost to package your product. This will include the materials cost, any printing costs, including printing your label, hang tab, and UPC barcode if needed, and the labor involved with kitting and packaging your individual product. Your packaging company may break out charges for boxes, picking and packing if you have more than one destination, warehousing, etc. So, be sure to ask them for all of the costs up front, including freight. To estimate the freight the company will need to know where you will be storing your product for shipment to your customers. This location could be your home, at a fulfillment center, warehouse, etc.

Insider secret: It will cost more to have your product shipped to your home because the shipping companies charge different rates for residential and commercial locations. Residential is most often higher, especially if you are shipping a lot of product and the shipper needs to have a special forklift to bring a pallet off the truck and into your driveway or garage.

If you're doing the packaging yourself, add up all of the costs for the materials, including the cost of mailing the materials to you and any sales taxes. Tell your vendors that you are a manufacturer, as they may have special pricing for you.

If you don't have it yet, break out your full packaging costs into per unit prices by dividing the total cost by the number of units you ordered.

For our example, let's assume these costs per unit are from your packaging quote:

- Packaging materials: $0.55
- Labor: $0.45
- Freight: $0.50
- Total Packaging Costs = $1.50

Add your cost to manufacture the product with your cost to package the product and you have your Cost of Goods Sold.

So for our example, the costs per unit of product sold are:

- Manufacturing: $3.50
- Packaging: $1.50
- Total Unit COGS = $5

Note that you may have additional costs depending on your situation and your distribution channel. For example, I add in a fulfillment fee that my fulfillment company charges me to ship my product. Sometimes you can pass that fee along to the customer in the mailing costs (i.e., the shipping and handling fees) but I do not so I can keep my customers' shipping costs down. Some people also break out the cost of freight into a separate item.

Now multiply the COGS by the number of units you will sell each month for each distribution channel:

- Online: 25 units x $5 COGS = $125
- Retail: 100 units x $5 COGS = $500
- Total COGS* = $625

COST OF GOODS SOLD

	Months												
	1	2	3	4	5	6	7	8	9	10	11	12	Total
Revenues by Channel													
Internet	$125	$125	$125	$125	$125	$125	$125	$125	$125	$125	$125	$125	$1500
Retail	$500	$500	$500	$500	$500	$500	$500	$500	$500	$500	$500	$500	$6000
Total COGS	$625	$625	$625	$625	$625	$625	$625	$625	$625	$625	$625	$625	$7500

*When you actually record your COGS, you will see that they fluctuate each month based on your gross revenues. For example purposes, we are estimating them to be the same each month.

Your Everyday Expenses (Fixed Costs)

Your everyday expenses are those expenses that you incur regardless of whether you sell any products or not. They're called fixed costs.

If you've started your business already, you know that there are recurring bills coming in each month, e.g., Web site hosting costs, monthly banking fee, etc. Other costs include things to run your office like utilities, telephone, rent, etc. If you are running your business from your home, you may be able to include portions of your personal utility, telephone, and other expenses. Check with your accountant for these percentages. Finally, you'll have set purchases that you make including office supplies, advertising, insurance, etc.

List of Fixed Expenses

Start adding up your monthly fixed costs. The list below is not an exhaustive list. I broke out the categories to get you thinking the costs you incur for your specific situation that may not be included in the sample list below. If you're comfortable with Excel, put this in a spreadsheet or search for "cash flow template" online and you'll find a number of existing templates to enter your fixed costs.

Put the monthly costs next to each category. Some costs may not occur every month, so for estimating purposes take your anticipated totals and divide by 12 months for the average. When you are filling out your actual cash flow, you can put the total amounts of, say, your advertising into the month or months you incur the costs.

Running Your Office:

- Supplies
- Payroll Expenses
- Repairs & Maintenance
- Vehicle Expenses
- Rent
- Telephone
- Utilities
- Mailing
- Computers/Equipment
- Other Office Costs: (Specify)

Purchases/Taxes:

- Outside Services
- Advertising
- Insurance
- Taxes (Real Estate, etc.)
- Trade Shows
- Travel
- Accounting & Legal
- Other Purchases: (Specify)

Sales Costs:

- Merchant Account
- Web Site
- Banking Fees
- Other Sales Costs: (Specify)

Add up your monthly fixed costs and enter it into your table. For the example, we'll estimate fixed costs at $275 a month. Don't be concerned if this is higher or lower than your actual fixed costs; as with all of the numbers, I am just using them as examples.

FIXED COSTS

Months

	1	2	3	4	5	6	7	8	9	10	11	12	Total
Fixed Expenses	$275	$275	$275	$275	$275	$275	$275	$275	$275	$275	$275	$275	$3300

Now, when we add all of the tables together, we'll have your projected income statement!

PROJECTED INCOME STATEMENT

Months

	1	2	3	4	5	6	7	8	9	10	11	12	Total
Gross Revenues by Channel													
Internet	$500	$500	$500	$500	$500	$500	$500	$500	$500	$500	$500	$500	$6000
Retail	$1000	$1000	$1000	$1000	$1000	$1000	$1000	$1000	$1000	$1000	$1000	$1000	$12000
Total Gross Revenues	$1500	$1500	$1500	$1500	$1500	$1500	$1500	$1500	$1500	$1500	$1500	$1500	$18000
Cost of Goods Sold													
Internet	$125	$125	$125	$125	$125	$125	$125	$125	$125	$125	$125	$125	$1500
Retail	$500	$500	$500	$500	$500	$500	$500	$500	$500	$500	$500	$500	$6000
Total COGS	$625	$625	$625	$625	$625	$625	$625	$625	$625	$625	$625	$625	$7500
Gross Profit	$875	$875	$875	$875	$875	$875	$875	$875	$875	$875	$875	$875	$10500
Fixed Expenses	$275	$275	$275	$275	$275	$275	$275	$275	$275	$275	$275	$275	$3300
Net Profits	$600	$600	$600	$600	$600	$600	$600	$600	$600	$600	$600	$600	$7200

You'll see two new line items gross and net profits. The gross profits are your gross revenues minus your cost of goods sold. When you subtract your fixed expenses from your gross profits, you'll get your net profits.

As promised, with your calculations you can begin doing any number of things.

Cash Flow: If you've started entering your fixed costs into a cash flow statement, you can add your estimated revenues and cost of goods sold to determine how much cash you will need to fund your company.

Inventory: With your estimations of units sold by channel in the revenues section, you can estimate how many units your manufacturer needs to make and when. In our example, calculating out the number of units needed each month equals 125 units (25 from Internet sales and 100 bought from your retailer). The yearly units needed are 1500, but if you're cash-strapped, you don't need necessarily need all of the units at the beginning of the year.

  If your manufacturer's lead time is 2 months, order an initial quantity where the price breaks are for your manufacturer. For example, if the cost at 250 units is $3.75 per unit and the cost at 500 units is $3.50 per unit, order 500 units 3 times per year instead of 250 units 6 times per year. You'll save $375 overall (i.e., $5625 - $5250 = $375). You will potentially have higher warehousing costs, but assess those against the production savings and determine the optimal choice.

Sales Goals: With your projected gross revenues, you can start comparing actual numbers to your forecasted sales number to assess how each of your channels of distribution is performing.

Caution! Once you start digging into the numbers, you may get addicted to estimating and calculating. And if you don't, at least you see how easy some of these financial spreadsheets really are.

Where to Get the Cash

Now that you have an estimate of how many units you might sell and the costs associated with making your product and running your office, you're getting a good idea of the cash needed to get your product to market.

Insider secret: Just about everything is going to cost more than you think. And it's going to take longer than you think. Be sure to add buffers into all of your projections.

If you haven't thought about it yet, now is the time to start considering where the money is going to come from. While everyone will tell you there are a number of traditional lending sources, I'm going to tell you the truth. There are really only a few funding options for the average small business that is just starting out. Now, if you have friends in high places or are launching the next great technology project, you will prove me wrong. But if you aren't building the next killer app and don't know any billionaires, don't despair. When you learn some of the insider secrets, you may decide that the traditional sources aren't for you anyway.

So, let's get started discussing some of the traditional and non-traditional sources of revenue.

Banks / Small Business Loans

Establishing a good relationship with a banker early on in your business journey is a good idea. They'll tell you things that you might not otherwise know. For instance, my banker told me that if I apply for a small business loan, I should submit the loan application to two or three banks at the same time. That's because credit scores won't be dinged as severely if all of the lenders check into your credit history within a three- or four-day period.

Banks will have a range of loan options for you. Most of the larger banks will have Small Business Association (SBA)-backed loans as well. Note that you don't get SBA loans directly from the SBA. The SBA works through banking partners. To make the loan to a small business more attractive for the bank, the SBA guarantees a portion of the loan to be paid back if the small company defaults on the loan.

You may be eligible for more than one type of loan, so be sure to review all of your options. There are special loans for qualifying businesses owned by women, minorities, and veterans.

The paperwork typically required for loan applications are:

- Application

- Personal Financial Statement

- Last 3 Years of Business Tax Returns (if applicable)

- Last 3 Years of Individual Tax Returns (if applicable)

- Year-to-Date Financial Statements (i.e., Income Statement & Balance Sheet)

- Verification of Liquidity (e.g., Bank Statements, Brokerage Statements, etc.)

- Documents to Support Business Structure (e.g., Articles of Incorporation, DBA, etc.)

- Personal Resume

- Business Plan

Conventional and SBA loans for small business are unsecured. That means the loan is not tied to any asset like your car or your home. An unsecured loan is based solely on the ability of the borrower to repay the loan. Banks and the SBA are looking for cash flow to be able to repay the loan. Let me say that again. Banks and the SBA are looking for *cash flow* to be able to repay the loan. That means they want to see that you're making money before they give you a loan.

If you are a sole proprietorship, the lenders may look at your personal household income. If you are incorporated, the lenders will look at your business income. What they're looking for in terms of being able to pay back the loan is the ratio between your incoming cash and your outgoing cash (i.e., debt service ratio). Typically, the SBA wants a debt service coverage of 1.25, which means for every $1.00 going out, you have $1.25 coming in. For conventional loans, the debt service coverage is higher, typically 1.50 to 1.75.

What this means is that no matter how great your big idea is, or how much potential income you are going to generate, lenders want to know how much money you're making right now—before you get the loan. It's a circular challenge; if you get funding, you'll be able to manufacture and sell the product, and thus create business income. But, you need the income first to qualify for the loan. In lots of cases, if you had the income to start with, you wouldn't need the loan!

Venture Capital

Ahhh venture capital. Just the words conjure up dreams of businesspeople in grey suits holding millions of dollars, just waiting for the opportunity to give it to some deserving small company. Okay, back to reality…

Venture capital is the cash from a private equity fund that venture capital firms provide to very high-potential companies. The fund is just money from other investors that is "managed" or invested by the venture capital firm.

In exchange for giving you the money, the venture capitalists will want a slice of the company. A big slice. Often, they bring more than just money, though. Through their networks, venture capitalists can supplement the leadership or financial expertise that a small business may be lacking. Why do they do this? It is in their best interest to make sure your venture succeeds. Many of the businesses that are invested in by venture capitalists are forecasted to grow very quickly. Explosive growth is difficult for small businesses, so seasoned professionals are brought in to help manage the inevitable challenges.

Venture capital is typically thought of in connection with technology companies because of its role in the Silicon Valley booms of the 1970s, 1980s, and 1990s. Venture capital firms do invest in a number of other industries as well, though.

The reason it is difficult for the typical small business to get this kind of funding is because the venture capital firms want to invest big money to get big returns—quickly. Consider if your product has the potential to make $5 million in the next 5 years. That's fantastic! But why would a venture capitalist firm want to invest in you? They usually don't make deals under $1 million. In fact, they typically invest millions of dollars over several rounds of financing with the goal of making multiple times that money in 3-5 years. Venture capital financing is often just too large for the average small business. But, hey, if you've got the right product, go for it. There's nothing better than getting a whole lot of funding (if you need it) and a whole lot of extra expertise (if you want it).

Angel Investments

The difference between a venture capitalist and an angel investor is that the angel is typically investing her or his own money into the venture directly. (Think *Shark Tank*). The advantage to the small business is that angel investors are able to make smaller investments than the venture capitalist. Angels often want a portion of your company as well, or they will work with the company for creative ways to gain the return on their investment.

More and more angel investors are joining networks of angel investors. This helps them get access to more deals and spread the risk around with other investors. Angel networks can be based in regions so that the investors can meet in person with each other and the potential firms. Finding the angel networks in your region is as easy as doing a Google search.

If you want to apply for funding from an angel network, you will need to have your ducks in a row. Each angel network has its own application process and requirements for paperwork and presentations. Some have application fees to weed out those companies that are just testing the waters.

While angel investors are typically associated with specific industries, that is changing. Angels often say they invest more in the person than in the product, so the industry in less important. What is important is the return on investment. Angels expect 10-30 times their investment typically within 3-5 years. That means if you get $75,000 in angel investing, the angel is expecting to make between $750,000 and $2,250,000. Yikes.

Because of that return on investment, angel financing is typically a second or third option for the startup company. Meaning you'll want to get startup funding from other sources at first, if possible. You may also want to wait a few years until you're established to seek angel funding as the investor(s) is going to look extensively at your financials to protect his or her investment.

Alternative Funding Sources

There are alternative forms of financing available to small businesses, too. I'm only mentioning two here because I'm wary of mentioning ones that are risky. Some alternative-financing sources offer real solutions for small companies that need funding but some are more risky and others are downright scams. Approach all financing options with a skeptical eye until you learn that they are safe and legitimate. The good news is that there are new trends in funding happening frequently; if you don't learn of one that works for you today, check around for something new to pop up tomorrow.

Crowd Funding

Crowd funding is just now making its way into the small business arena. Usually associated with charity or artistic works, crowd funding is a way to get donations from a bunch of regular people (e.g., "the crowd") via the Internet. Why it is important to you is because more and more small companies are using these sites not to garner donations, but to get funding and often pre-sell their products. In exchange for providing cash that the small company can use for product development and manufacturing, the company will give some contributors the completed product once it's ready. Some companies establish different contribution levels (e.g., some contributors only receive small items like T-shirts), which make it easy for the small company to garner a larger crowd of funders without having to give a product to each contributor. Check out kickstarter.com and peerbackers.com for more information on this.

Accounts Receivable Financing

If you're really in a bind, some lenders will give you a loan based on your accounts receivables and some even on purchase orders. Think of it this way, you receive a big order from your retail buyer but you don't have enough inventory to cover the order. So, you need to do a production run. But you don't have enough cash on hand to finance another run at this time. So, what do you do?

These lenders may give you the funding, secured by the order from your buyers, so that you can pay your manufacturer, who may want you to purchase your inventory upfront. This especially happens when you are working with overseas manufacturers. When the buyer pays you, you repay the lender. In some cases the lender requires that your buyer sends the money directly to the lender.

Think of it like a pay-day loan for business—it's money now instead of having to wait for your buyer to pay you. It can be costly and it may send a negative impression to your buyer if they are required to send your payment to your lender, but it is an option if you are in a bind.

Self-Financing

I left self-financing for last. It's probably the place you'll need to start first.

If I were telling my best friend about this, I'd tell her to keep her job for as long as possible so she can finance the early stages of her company, like the product development stage, herself. Unless you get outside funding, the reality is that you're probably not going to be able to pay yourself for a good year or two. That's a double strike if you leave a job—first, you're not getting a pay check and second, you've got to fund your early-stage company somehow. If you're using your savings for the company, you won't have them to replace your income.

If you're not in a position of having or keeping a job, you may have to start with funding from your savings, retirement accounts, home equity loan, family, or friends. And eat macaroni and cheese for the foreseeable future. If you are passionate about your product, the macaroni and cheese won't taste so bad.

Financial To Dos

Before we leave the financial section, if you haven't already, do two important things:

1. Hire a small business accountant.

You may only think about accountants at tax time. Or, if you do your own taxes, you may not ever think about accountants. As you start and grow your company, you really should consider finding one that you like and trust. That's because accountants who work with small businesses, in particular, often have a wealth of information and contacts that can be invaluable to you. Beyond helping you determine your tax-paying designation and filing what can be complicated taxes, these accountants can introduce you to bankers, lawyers, other entrepreneurs, bookkeeping resources, and more. They can be skittish about giving advice, but often they'll share what they know because in many cases they are small business owners themselves.

2. Purchase an accounting software package to start tracking your costs and revenues.

If you're just starting out and don't have a lot of expenses to track yet, you may think accounting software is not necessary. However, especially when you're focusing on product development, managing vendors, and invoicing customers, it is very easy to lose track of small details.

Even if you are very organized and have a system for managing your expenses and sales, an accounting software package can organize, analyze, and output your data into helpful information about the health of your company. For example, the software package can tell you how much sales tax you owe to your state, which vendors still haven't paid their invoices, and which months are the best sales months for your products. It can tell you how much you're spending on advertising versus your Cost of Goods Sold and how much inventory you have left. Depending on the software you choose, it may even help you with payroll functions when the time comes to hire employees. Additionally, by using financial software you'll be better prepared at tax time and your small business accountant will really like you.

Some of the most popular packages for small business are Sage PeachTree and QuickBooks. Depending on the version, the software likely will cost you a few hundred dollars. The software companies typically offer online training and there are many independent trainers for the most popular options, if you feel you need more hands-on instruction.

How Are You Going to Pay For It? Checklist

❑ Forecast your sales by selecting conservative, crazy, and middle-of-the road estimates

❑ Estimate the costs to make and package your products based on your manufacturing and packaging quotes

❑ Calculate your everyday expenses based on either actual bills or estimated costs

❑ Consider your funding options

❑ Hire a small business accountant

❑ Purchase accounting software to start tracking your costs and revenues.

What Would You Tell Your Best Friend About... MONEY?

Keep their day job while transitioning to working full-time in their business—once they have actual clients and income coming in from their solo venture then they can resign from their day job knowing how much income they have coming in from their dream job. This will take a lot of the financial pressure off them and will make their new venture a pleasant experience.

Brooke Guthrie, Owner
Mama Earth Rocks Publishing
www.mamaearthrocks.com

My one big piece of advice is that you want to have complete control of your idea from start to finish, so your equity is key in the direction of the business.

Craig Wolfe, President
CelebriDucks
www.CelebriDucks.com

Learn basic accounting procedures—very basic—so that you can keep things straight. Draft a budget within a month or two. Worry about the structure of your business—sole proprietor or corporation—later, much later. Timing your business, your brand, and your product is important—very important— and you should consult experts about it.

Robert Ellis Smith, Publisher
PRIVACY JOURNAL
www.privacyjournal.net

Chapter 8:
How to Get Noticed

Yea! Getting noticed by customers is my favorite topic and something I've learned to do very cheaply. Luckily in this age of social media, reaching customers has never been cheaper. And every single entrepreneur out there knows it, too. So, you guessed it, it's getting harder and harder to get noticed.

Unless you're doing the right things.

In this chapter, I'll go over some of the best things you can be doing right now to get awareness for your product. I want to focus primarily on the new types of marketing tools. But there are traditional tools which may be viable solutions for you, too. They are typically more costly, so I'm going to recommend you focus on what you can do for as little cost as possible, at least in the beginning.

As a former marketing professional, I would be remiss if I didn't mention your overall marketing strategy. Yes, you need one and while I talk about objectives and strategy in relation to social media, in this book I decided to focus on the key sites and tools you can start using right now.

Start from the Start

The first place to start is with your Web site. As soon as a customer gets interested in your product, he or she is going to go to your Web site. And if you're selling your product on the site, your customer should be able to immediately find your product(s) on the home page. Your home page is not the home page of a large corporation where they have the luxury of talking for paragraph after paragraph about themselves, their customers, and how much they love their employees.

No, your home page is a store front. It delivers what your customers want as soon as they arrive on the page. Your product(s) are showcased right up front, as close to the top of the page as possible. Potential customers should be able to see the product they came for and be one click away from getting to all of the details and the order-now opportunity.

That said, even if you have only one product, only give the customer enough copy on the home page to intrigue them into clicking onto a second page. You may only have one chance with this customer and your goal is to get them to linger on your site long enough to buy. If your customer lands on your home page and bounces right off, you're going to lose that sale.

Your secondary pages can include "About us," "Contact us," and other information.

Search Engine Optimization

Make your site searchable by the top search engines by including Meta tags and keywords in the HTML source codes.

The Meta tags and keywords should include phrases and words that your customers are searching on. You may think you know what keywords to select right off the bat. You may not know how your customers think about (and therefore, search for) your product, though.

To find the keywords that your customers are searching on, use a keyword tool to estimate traffic and the popularity of a word or phrase. Keyword tools will tell you how many people have typed that search word or phrase into search engine forms in the past month.

When you arrive at the tool, type the word or phrase that you first think of for your product into the search box and see how many searches have been made. The keyword tool will also give you the results for words and phrases slightly altered, so you can see what other searches have been made. Keep trying different words and phrases until you have a clear idea of how people are searching for your type of product.

If your Web site interface allows you to add these words yourself, add the most popular words or phrases to the HTML code on your home and product pages. Make sure to also include these keywords in the copy on your pages. The search engines like it best when the page content and the keywords are in alignment.

Product Demonstration Videos

Video is a great way to draw visitors to your site. Google is having a love affair with video, so if you include video on your site, your site will rank higher in the Google search results. Be sure to post your video on YouTube.com, as well, with links back to your site.

Video is also a great way to demonstrate your product right from the Internet. It's almost like you're speaking with customers one-on-one when you're able to show them how your product works through video.

Pay-Per-Click Advertising

To bring customers to your site, you could create a pay-per-click (PPC) campaign. Both Google and Facebook will guide you through the process of creating an online advertisement that will show up at the top or in the sidebars of the Google or Facebook sites. There are other types of PPC ads and platforms, but Google and Facebook are the most popular.

Google AdWords

The objective of a Google AdWords advertisement is to get potential customers to click on the ad, which will then bring them to your Web site.

To create the ad, write a few lines of copy and the Google Adwords' wizard will tell you how many characters your ad can have. Google Adwords also provides tips and videos on how to write a great ad.

The next step is to select your keywords. Each keyword has a different cost-per-click based on the competition for the word. If you tried a keyword tool earlier for your Web site tags, did you notice the columns that said "Competition" and "Approximate CPC?" Those columns relate to online ads. If competition is high, the cost you will pay when someone clicks on your ad, or the approximate cost-per-click (CPC), will be higher than the average. For example, the phrase "cat litter" has high competition. If I wanted to create an ad and use cat litter as one of my keywords, it would cost me approximately $1.76 every time someone clicked on the ad. In contrast, the phrase "world's best cat litter" has lower competition and would cost me $1.22 for every click.

Once your ad is written and your keywords are selected, you can choose how long your ad will run. You can decide if you want it to run for a certain length of time, for an indefinite length of time with a capped per-day budget, or for as long as it can with a lifetime budget.

Google Adwords provides analytics to tell you the performance of your overall campaigns and drills down into other key metrics, so you can make changes for weak performing ads or keywords. Google adds new features to Adwords' metrics frequently.

Facebook

The objective of a Facebook advertisement is to get potential customers to "like" your company's or product's Facebook page (described below). Facebook is a little more generous with the amount of words you can have with your ad. It also automatically recommends a photograph from the images on your Facebook company or product page, but you can change the ad if you'd like.

Choosing which demographics you'd like your Facebook ad to reach is quite easy. If you want to reach only <u>women</u> in the <u>US</u> who like <u>cooking</u>, you can click on those three attributes and a neat tool on the left side of the advertisements page will show you how many people are in that category on Facebook.

Facebook uses information your potential customers have supplied in their profiles, as well as updates from their personal status pages, to provide that demographic data.

When you have created your ad and selected your demographics, you can set a per-day budget or a lifetime budget. Similarly to Google Adwords, your ad will then run continuously, for a specified time, or for a specified budget.

While pay-per-click campaigns are relatively easy and fun to set up, they really are an art form unto themselves. Professionals study the habits of Internet users to determine the right combinations of words, time of day, day of week, etc. to yield the best campaign results. If you are not receiving enough site visitors from your campaign, try one of the hundreds of agencies dedicated to this type of advertising. They may be able to help you achieve your desired results.

The Wide Wide World of Social Media

Everybody and her brother have written tomes about social media. If you don't know what it is, it's basically interactive communication on the Web. It includes Facebook, Twitter, blogs, Web site contests, YouTube, LinkedIn, Wikipedia, WikiAnswers, Pinterest, epinions.com, and dozens and dozens of other sites and applications and types of communication vehicles. If that brief description doesn't give you an idea of what this vast new world includes, think about it with the broad definition of "consumer-generated media" and that may help clarify.

Below are descriptions of some of the most popular, current social media sites and tools.

Facebook Product Pages

In addition to your personal profile page, Facebook enables you to create a business page. One distinction with the two is that on your personal page, people "friend" you. On your business page, people "like" you. Additionally, your business page gives you many sections in addition to your status to promote your business.

When you post on your product page, your updates will show up on all of the personal profile pages of the people who "like" you. That means by posting, you are reaching more than just your direct community members, but potentially hundreds of additional potential customers.

You can even begin selling right from your product page. Facebook has a marketplace, but this is more like a classified ad section. What you really want is a Facebook store. Your store appears in your product page's left-hand navigation bar similar to your photos. If potential customers link on your store, they will be directed to a product page within the Facebook store. If they click an order button, they will be taken to your Web site and shopping cart to finish the ordering process. Facebook doesn't yet have its own application to create your store; other developers have created applications to get your store easily up and running. Mine is a free application through my Web site hosting company, Volusion.

Insider secret: You can choose which section a new visitors land on when they arrive at your Facebook product page. Selecting your store is a good way to get your product in front of potential customers who may just be browsing around.

Cost: Free; but you may have to pay someone to create your store.

STIKITTY'S FACEBOOK PRODUCT PAGE

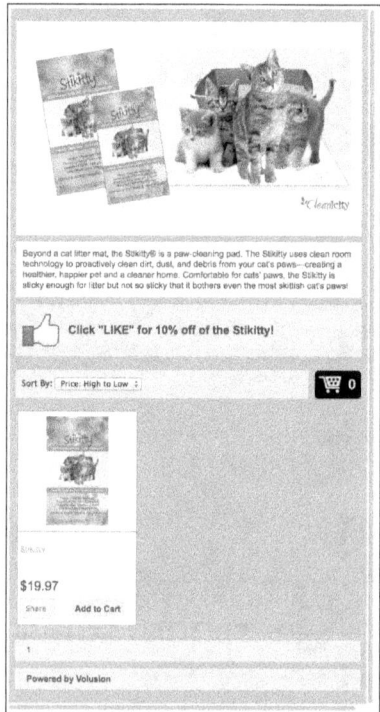

STIKITTY'S FACEBOOK STORE

Twitter

"Tweets" are 140-character quick updates that people post on Twitter.com. These updates frequently have a more business-oriented tone than Facebook status updates, but not always. Twitter allows people with like interests to follow each other, meaning they can see each other's tweets in their update lists.

The advantage to Twitter is that your posts are public; hence the more business-like tone. That means you can send mini-press release information out about your company to your followers and anyone who searches on the topic of your tweet. One person can easily "re-tweet" your message if they like it, and it will show up in the status updates of all the people following them.

Tweets can include links, which can be shortened at Web sites like bitly.com. You'll want to shorten your links, so they don't take up too much of or even the entire 140-character limit. Twitter automatically shortens the links now, but they still appear long and unattractive. Try it and you'll see what I mean.

Real-time feedback on events or happenings is becoming a very popular thing for Twitter. While sitting in a seminar, people can tweet what the speaker is saying. It allows for content to be spread around faster and easier than ever before. Some of it is nonsense too, like people tweeting about something some reality-show character just said on the latest episode.

If you take the good with the bad, Twitter can be a great promotional tool for your product.

Cost: Free

Pinterest

What does your small business have to do with the sharing of favorite things like arts and crafts and recipes? Why, Pinterest, of course.

Pinterest is a social media site dedicated to bringing people together through shared interests. Members share photos and other media by pinning it to their "image board" (think digital cork board). Other members can re-pin these favorite items and share them with their friends. If you or another member pin your product image, and then others re-pin it, information about your product can quickly spread throughout the community. It's a great way to get people "talking" about your product for free!

Insider secret: Be careful on Pinterest to include more than just your own product. Too much self-promotion will turn the Pinterest community off quickly. Balance information on your product with sharing other things that might interest the community. This is a good reminder for all of your social media interactions.

Cost: Free

Blogs

If Twitter is a mini-press release for your product, a blog is more like a full-length infomercial. Blogs are articles written by various experts or non-experts on topics that interest them. Some blogs are rambling muses and others are in-depth essays. Most are something in-between. Perhaps more than any other social media vehicle, a blog typically has a specific and consistent purpose. They educate, inform, entertain, or update their readers.

If you use your blog carefully, you can discuss your product or business in a way that doesn't seem like pure promotion, which tends to turn readers off.

One caution is that blogs take a considerable amount of time to maintain. To keep people interested and following your blog, you need to post frequently. At least on a weekly basis! To make it a little easier to post, some of the blog sites allow you to post via email or your smart phone.

Wordpress and Tumblr are some of the leading sources for creating your blog.

Cost: Free, unless you want add-ons like video-hosting capabilities

Contests

There are several different types of contests for small businesses which will create exposure for you and your product. If you enter a contest, the site usually posts a profile on you and your product. Visitors to the site get to vote on the profiles and products they like the most. This is a great way to get your product in front of thousands of potential customers.

StartUpNation.com offers contests for home-based businesses, women-owned businesses and more. Other sites offer prizes with their contests including money for your business, promotional services, product giveaways, and more.

Cost: Usually free

Product Reviews

Having a third-party review and endorse your product can be a very valuable tool for promoting your product. You can ask an expert or even a blogger with credibility in your product area.

Potential customers might read right over your promotional material, but often will read an expert's review with eagerness.

For example, when I first started selling the Stikitty®, I was often asked whether it bothered cats' paws. I tested and revised the product's tackiness several times until we achieved the right balance. No matter how often I explained this to some customers, a few of them still hesitated. Then a cat behaviorist approached me and offered to test the stickiness of the Stikitty® with multiple cats, some more skittish than others. Her reviewed showed that the Stikitty® was successful in grabbing the litter without impacting the cats. To many of my customers, her review was more important than anything I could have said. I still get asked today about whether cats mind the stickiness and immediately I point them to my Web site to read the study from the expert.

To have a blogger or an expert review your product, it can be as simple as asking. Put together a list of bloggers who post on your industry and send them an email. In the email, explain your product and ask them if they would like a free copy of the product in exchange for a product review. Don't hesitate to ask because it's a win-win all the way around. Reviewers get content for their blogs and you get your product in front of everyone who visits their Web site. I can tell you that in the beginning, one product review sent more potential customers to my site than any other promotional effort.

Many established bloggers are doing something interesting. They are combining posts, contests, and product reviews to help get the social buzz going on products. Similar to a regular review, they receive a sample and post a review. They also offer a chance for a lucky reader to receive a second sample. Typically, all the reader has to do is comment on the blog, follow your product on Twitter, like your Facebook page, or make some other social media connection.

Cost: typically a few samples; rarely some of the blogger contests require you to pay a fee for your product to be included in the review

Video-Sharing Sites

Just like other content-generating sites, sites like YouTube.com and Metacafe.com allow you to post your own content, except this time the content is videos. The videos are open to the public. As mentioned earlier, while you can have product demos on your site also put them on video-sharing sites. Most of the sites allow you to post your videos for free. Once live, you can then embed the link from their site into other locations like your Web site or blog.

Cost: Free on many sites

Your Social Media Strategy and More

Despite the overabundance of information about how to be successful with social media, it really comes down to one word:

Post.

If you don't post, you won't get seen. If you're not seen, no one will know about your product and therefore no one will buy your product.

Okay, so where should you post? You could take all day and still not leverage all of the opportunities you have to get noticed using social media. If you want to get anything else done during the day, you will have to narrow down your efforts and having a strategy is a must.

As with all of your business activities, start with your objective. What do you want to accomplish? If you're like most small businesses, your primary objective is to sell more products, but see if you can be more specific. For example, if I were stating an objective for my new pet massager product, I might say, "I want to sell 50 pet massagers in three months through my social media efforts."

How I would do that is my strategy. My strategy is the path I will take to achieve my objective. I've already chosen social media as my channel, but I can narrow that down to how I will use that channel to sell my product. And, because social media is best when it is an interaction, I can involve other people in my strategy. As my strategy example, I might say, "I will offer a discount to new customers through pet bloggers to achieve my objective."

I have an objective of selling 50 pet massagers and a path, or strategy, of offering a discount via pet bloggers. Now I need to set some goals. My goals will break down the objective into action steps. For example, "I need to get 10 pet bloggers to talk about my pet massager; I need each of those bloggers to reach at least 100 potential customers; I need to convert 5% of those potential customers into buyers using my discount.

Now that I have goals, I can start putting tactics (i.e., "to dos") around them. For my example, my tactics might sound like this, "To achieve my objective in three months, I have to:

- Month One: decide on my discount level, reach out to the bloggers, and potentially send out samples

- Month Two: use all of my social media interactions to discuss my new pet massage and drive potential customers to the bloggers who are talking about my product

- Month Three: reach out to the people interested in my product from the bloggers' sites and sell them my product or at least connect with them via social media channels."

While this is a simple example, defining what you want to achieve and then using your social media interactions to both overtly and subtly drive toward your objective will help you make the most of your time spent with social media.

As an exercise, see if you can complete the following for your own product within the context of your social media efforts:

Objective: I want…

Strategy: I will…

Goals: I need to…

Tactics: I have to…

Press Releases

I did say I wasn't going to focus on the traditional forms of marketing. However, I think press releases are a good discussion topic, especially because they can get your product noticed and you can distribute them for free!

Sites like free-press-release.com, PR.com, and a dozen other press release sites allow you to upload your press release and deliver it through the Web for free. For a small fee, they will also send it to specialized media outlets for you.

If you've never written a press release, you'll want to learn how to write one to take full advantage of the exciting things coming up for you. You can write one to tell people that you've started your business; your Web site is up; you've launched your product, etc.

Good press releases have a standard format:

- Headline: Strong headlines grab the reader's attention in only a few seconds; headlines that include numbers or percentages are powerful; include your company name in the headline to add credibility

- Summary: the summary is an important overview of what's in the press release; if the reader likes it, they will continue reading further so put a lot of thought into your summary

- Date and Location

- Body: the first paragraph really has to tell the whole story in just a few sentences. The rest of the body copy explains the first paragraph in more detail

- Boilerplate: boilerplate copy is the information about your company. "XYZ, based in Boston, MA, was founded in 20XX…its premier product, the ZYX…"

- Contact Information.

If you're not comfortable writing a press release, find a press release for a similar story and see how the writer has structured her or his press release. You can structure yours in the same way. Once you have done it a few times, you'll gain the confidence to write and send out press releases that get noticed!

If you're concerned that you won't get noticed because the distribution service is free, I will share a story. When I first launched the Stikitty®, I wrote a press release about it and sent it out through 6 or 7 free press release services. A blogger in my town saw my release online and asked me if he could interview me for a blog story. I said, of course! Within a day after the blog was posted, a reporter from NBC-TV read the blog story and contacted me for an on-air interview!

Example of Using a Free Press Release Service to Get Noticed in Larger Publications

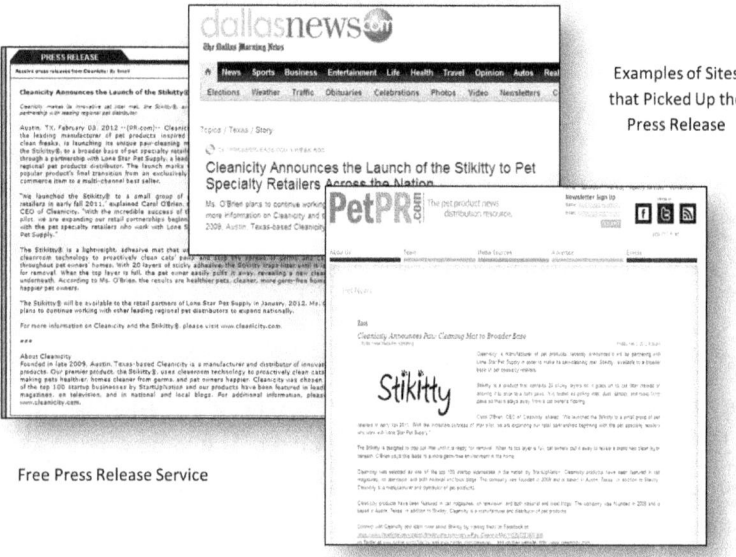

Examples of Sites
that Picked Up the
Press Release

Free Press Release Service

How to Get Noticed Checklist

- ❑ Launch your Web site (a.k.a your store front)

- ❑ Optimize your site for search engines

- ❑ Promote your product with a product demonstration video

- ❑ Promote your product with Pay-Per-Click ads

- ❑ Define your social media objective, strategy, goals, and tactics

- ❑ Post!

- ❑ Create a Facebook product page

- ❑ Create and post to a Twitter account

- ❑ Blog (if you have time to do it consistently!)

- ❑ Enter startup and small business contests

- ❑ Get your product reviewed by an expert or a blogger in your industry

- ❑ Send out press releases—as often as possible.

What Would You Tell Your Best Friend About... PASSION?

If you truly feel it inside you, and you're in tune with it, you can't go wrong. Because the road is long and hard and the only thing you will have with you is that feeling inside, make sure it's strong.

Rachana Suri, Founder
Accessuri
Accessuri.com

Every single time, I will encourage them to jump in and have fun while doing it. I always share with them that there will always be ups and downs, things will take three times as long as you think and cost twice as much, that's part of getting used to doing business. But...in the end, it's all worth it.

I believe every one of us in the world has a mission and a purpose and it's our duty to share it with the world.

Be passionate and stay focused. If you stick with it and have a true mission to add value to the world, it will come and you'll love it.

Ely Delaney, Founder
Your Marketing University
www.YourMarketingUniversity.com

About the Author

Carol O'Brien is the founder and president of Cleanicity, a consumer products company that makes pet products inspired by clean freaks. The company was selected by Startupnation.com as one of the 100 leading home-based businesses for two years in a row. Its premier product, the Stikitty®, is cleaning the paws of cats all over the US and making the homes of cat owners cleaner and healthier. The company is currently working on two additional products for dogs.

In addition to being a founder and an entrepreneur, Carol has an MBA in entrepreneurship and marketing from the number-one college for entrepreneurship, Babson College. Carol's career includes working on the digital marketing campaigns of branding giants such as American Express, Bausch & Lomb, Motorola, and Xerox. Additionally, she held senior-level marketing positions in financial and professional services companies. The entrepreneurial bug was strong even then, and eventually Carol had had enough of the corporate world and launched her company. And her happiness.

Now, in addition to creating products, Carol has found a passion for helping fellow entrepreneurs and business owners achieve their own success. She's been interviewed by NBC-TV and CreateChatterTV. She's written and has been featured in numerous articles and blogs on entrepreneurship.

www.ingramcontent.com/pod-product-compliance
Lightning Source LLC
Chambersburg PA
CBHW072026190526
45166CB00015B/514